12 Solo Guitar P

Grade 2- Grade 6 Level
with downloadable audio

Hi and welcome to 12 Solo Guitar pieces. This book is designed to give you a way of expanding your repertoire of solo pieces whilst simultaneously working on specific areas of musicianship.

I found a lot of the repertoire for guitar at the early stages didn't make use of the full guitar neck and range of the guitar, a lot of the examination pieces tended to stick withing the first few frets of the guitar. These pieces from the start extend across more of the guitar neck and aim to be more full sounding whilst still not being technically impossible for the developing guitarist. Each piece is full sounding on its own so can be performed or played just for pleasure. The compositions are of varying difficulty (Between grade 2 and grade 6 level).

While the criteria for pieces of certain levels may vary from these, the grades reflect the technical difficulty level.

For the more advanced student, the easier pieces are still relevant as they focus on elements of musicianship that are applicable to all levels.

I hope you have a lot of fun learning and playing the pieces!

David

www.daveseries.com

Copyright © 2024 David Series
All rights reserved.
ISBN: 979-8-8780-8697-4

QR CODE FOR AUDIO DOWNLOAD
(also available at www.daveseries.com)

CONTENTS

1) **Seven Hills (Grade 2/3 Level)** 3
   Focus - Melody and projection

2) **Island Sands - (Grade 3 Level)** 7
   Focus - Groove

3) **Nostalgic - (Grade 3 Level)** 12
   Focus - Tuning, dynamics and accents

4) **Last Embers - (Grade 3/4 Level)** 16
   Focus - Legato Playing

5) **Aragón (Grade 4 Level)** 21
   Focus - Harmony (chord construction)

6) **Bongo Bobi (Grade 4 level)** 29
   Focus - Rhythmic accuracy and subdivisions

7) **Glow (Grade 3 Level)** 34
   Focus - Chordal playing technique

8) **Quirky (Grade 5 level)** 38
   Focus - Melodic Minor scale and harmony

9) **Twisted Blue (Grade 5/6 level)** 42
   Focus - Rhythm (Triplet feel)

10) **Pepe of Granada (Grade 3/4 level)** 46
    Focus - Phrasing

11) **Shady (Grade 5)** 50
    Focus - Modal playing and theory

12) **Coloured Stones (Grade 7)** 55
    Focus - Right-Hand Tremelo

1) Seven Hills (Grade 2 Level)

Right-Hand Technique

Study 1a

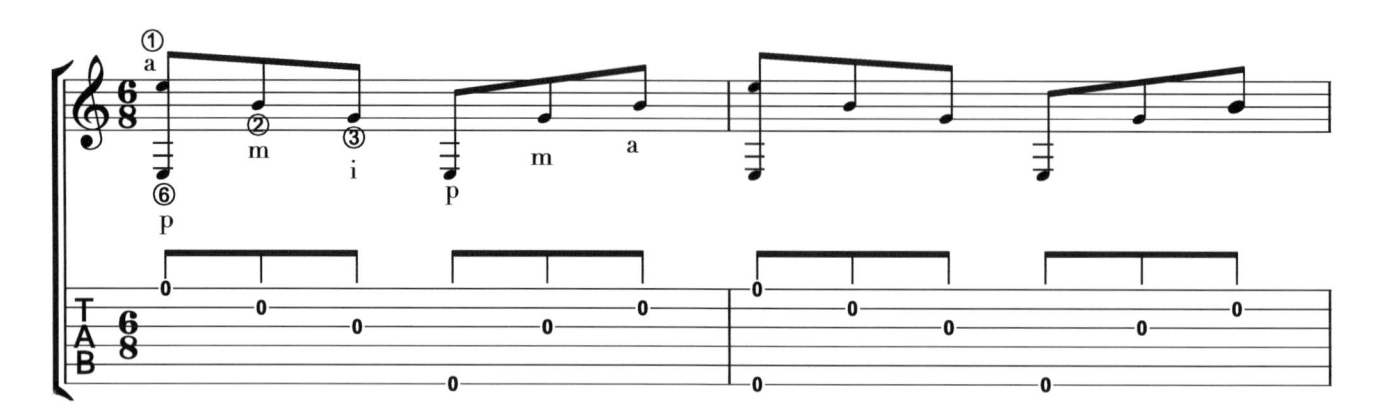

The right hand technique is often neglected in guitarists. In many styles, developing this technique can really open up your playing and give you much more control and fluency to play (Flamenco, Brazilian, Classical, Jazz, Country, Ragtime and many more).

This is a simple study to develop use of the four fingers in the right hand which are used most often: p, i , m, a. (Pulgar, Indice, Medio, Anular). The right-hand pinky is not used as much but can be represented by 'c', meaning Chiquito.

Some things to try and be aware of while practising this study:

- Breathing….are you aware of your breath….try not to hold your breath or breathe from the upper part of your chest. Breathe into your belly……let it out!

- Right-hand fingers, wrist and arm as relaxed and loose as possible. In fact, all of your body as relaxed as possible. This isn't always possible but try to aspire to that feeling when practising. Even take a minute….or five… at that start of your practice session to sit and just breathe…..keep coming back to your breath and let your body relax…….you can do this at the end of your practice session too. I find going super slow through some scales, or a piece that I know really well, helps me to focus on letting my body relax and breath.

- Correct alignment of fingers: One trick to get the right hand into the correct position is to put all fingers on the 1st String. So: p,i,m,a all lined up next to each other. Then, from there, move one at a time to the relevant strings for this exercise. So 'p' goes to 6th String, 'i' goes to 3rd string and 'm' to the 2nd strings.

- First try this exercise without a metronome to get used to where your fingers need to be, then play for a couple of minutes with a metronome on each of the six beats, maybe 80 bpm. Slowly increase the speed day by day…if it feels messy and out of control or tense then lower the speed and work on that for a bit longer until it feels like you have control over playing it without needing to think too much or try too hard.

- If your just starting out with focusing on right-hand technique then just keep trying, be patient, stick to the correct fingerings and techniques and eventually it will become easier!

Seven Hills Melody- Study1b

Before we start the full arrangement of this piece, let's try looking at the main melody alone. Playing the melody like this (before worring about all the fingerings, different strings at once etc.) means that when you come to add the other parts, your ear will be tuned in to the melody and it should sound stronger and project much more clearly on top of the other parts. When playing through this study:

- Give each note its full rhythmic value i.e. In this piece see if you can count 6 all the way through. It might be easier to clap the notes and count out loud before you try playing….This is a good habit to develop for players of any level, whatever the complexity of the music.

- Project your sound…Imagine there is someone sitting on the other side of your flat/ house/ school and try to project the melody to them….this doesn't mean you need to press hard with your left hand or pull the strings loudly with your right hand, it's more about trying to let the sound fill the room/ space. Recording yourself is another exercise you could try to help with this.

Study 1b

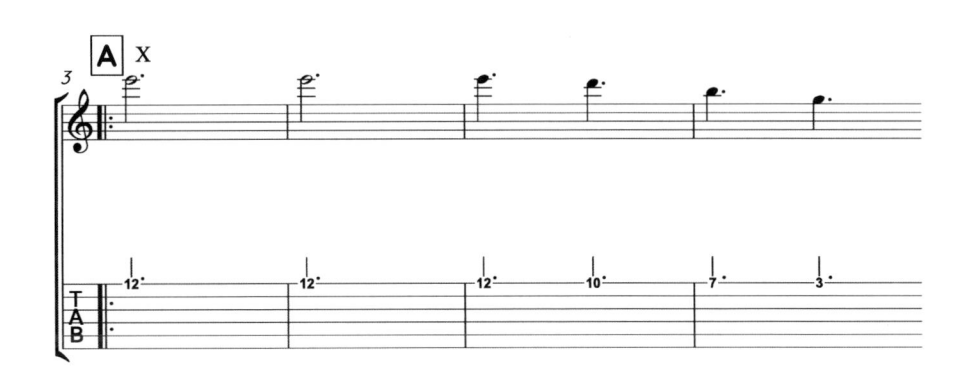

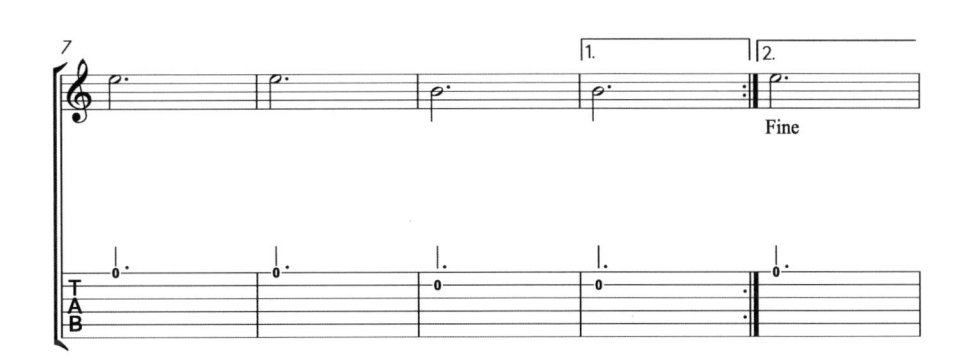

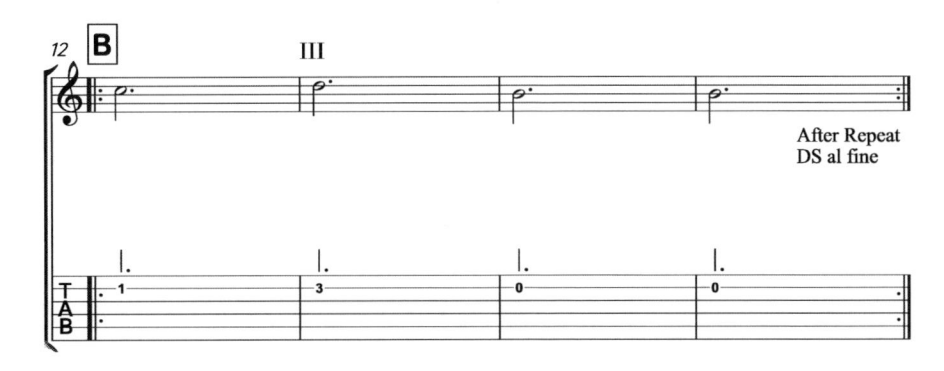

Seven Hills

Expressivo [♩.=65-80]

David Series

Seven Hills (Continued)

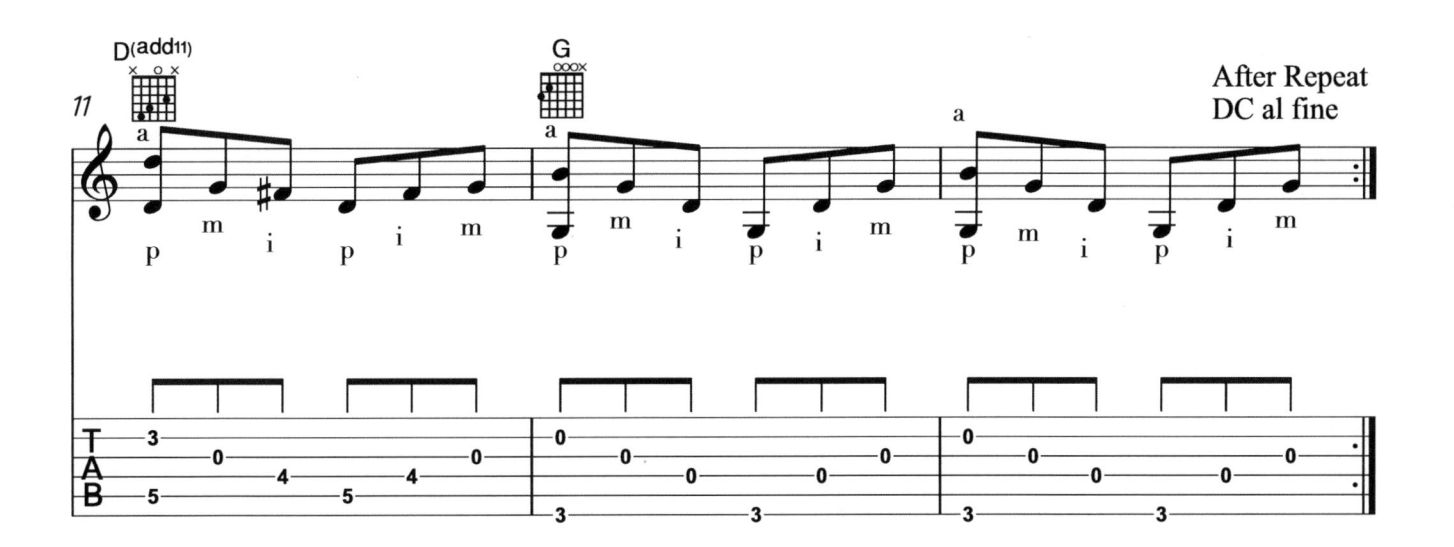

2) Island Sands (Grade 3 Level)

Groove

Study 2a

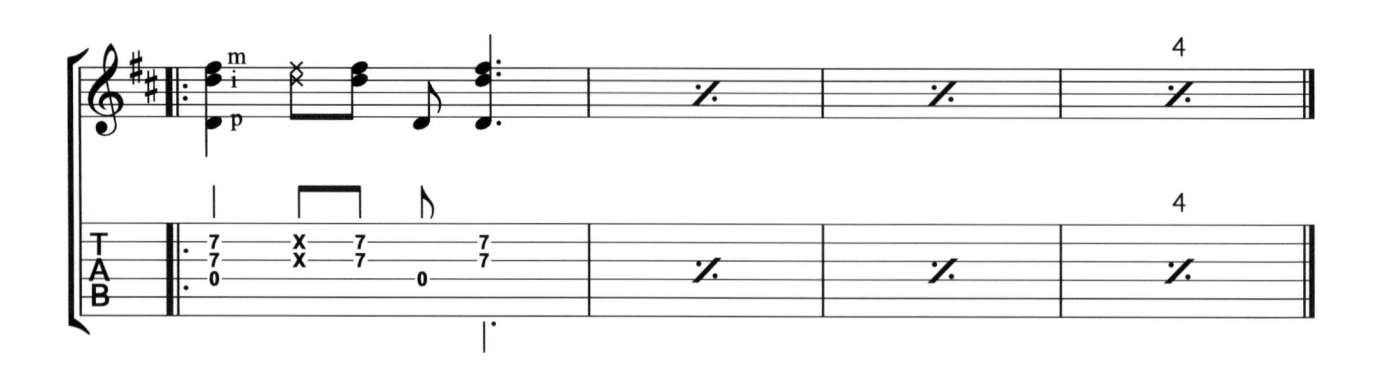

Here we begin to look at playing more rhythmically.

- The right hand of a guitarist is like your very own rhythm section, the drums or percussion. This is just a one bar rhythmic pattern and should be learnt on its own first before getting into the complexities of tricky fingerings and fret positions etc. Once you have learnt this and can play it round and round without reading the music then we can move on to the piece.

- I think it's a great thing to do to keep referring back to the groove whilst learning the piece. So say for example you have worked on the first four bars, you can now try playing four bars of the groove and then four bars of the piece. This is quite similar to how Flamenco musicians play and learn their music.

- This idea can be used in most pieces as a method of practising i.e. looping a one or two bar vamp/ groove pattern and alternating between that and small sections of the piece you're practising. This way you keep developing the groove and rhythmic flow of the piece as well as just the notes.

- Can you play the riff for 30 seconds staying relaxed?.........for 1 minute?.....2 Minutes? The guitar is such an interesting instrument, it can be easily to let your concentration waiver and when you feel the urge to play something else…see if you can play this study or something similar and simple for a short period of time without playing anything else, try to breathe and stay relaxed. Then you are practising a different thing to the notes, you're working on the groove or flow, and the rhythm of the phrase.

Accents

Now you can play the groove of this piece, the next step is to try and vary the accents (an accented note is slightly louder and more pronounced than the others, using the '>' symbol about or below the note or chord). Experiment with accenting different parts of the riff. It can be really effective accenting certain parts. Next time you listen to some music, a soloist or band, try to hear where the accents are and how they affect the music. Below are a few suggestions of varying the accent in this piece, which placement do you prefer?!

Study 2b

Island Sands

Brightly
[♩=120-130]

David Series

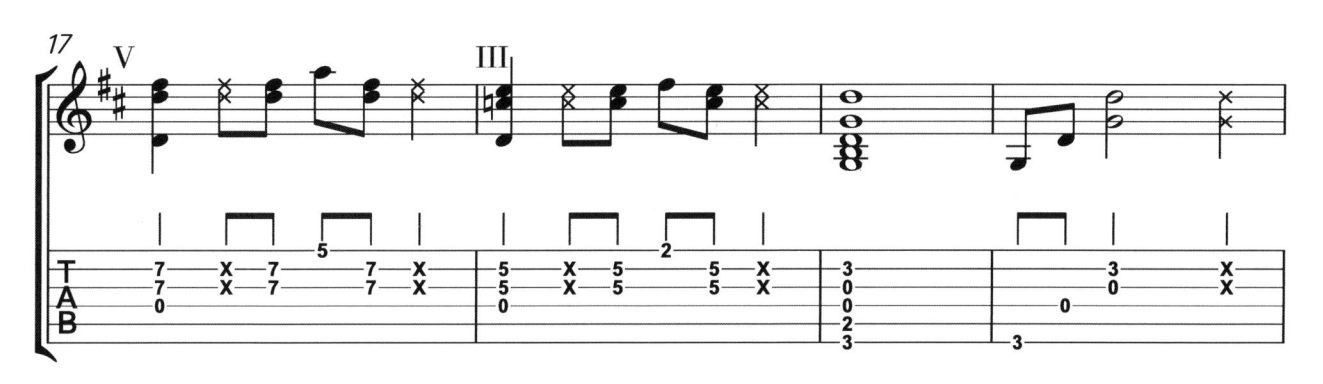

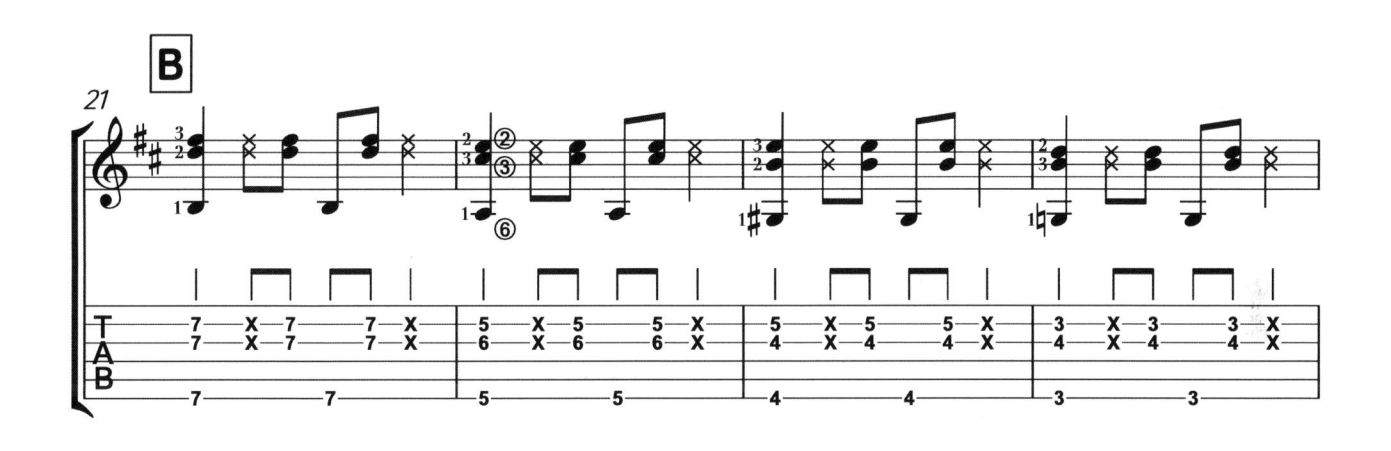

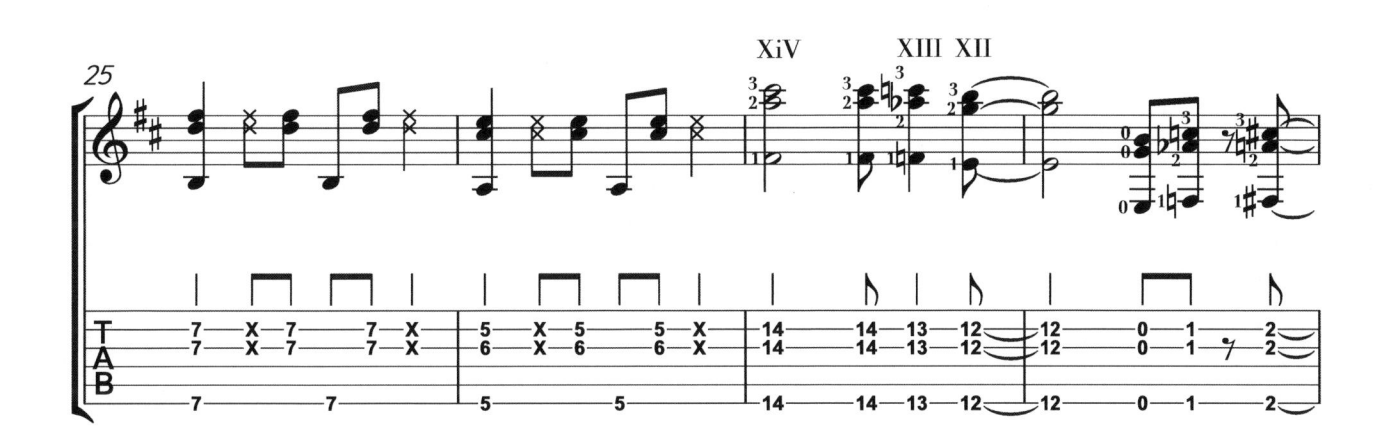

Island Sands (P2)

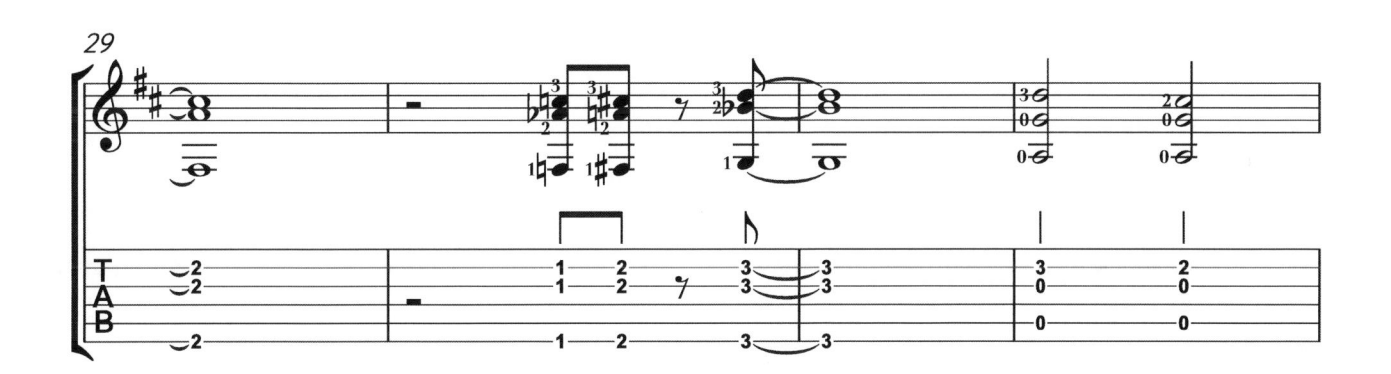

Island Sands (P3)

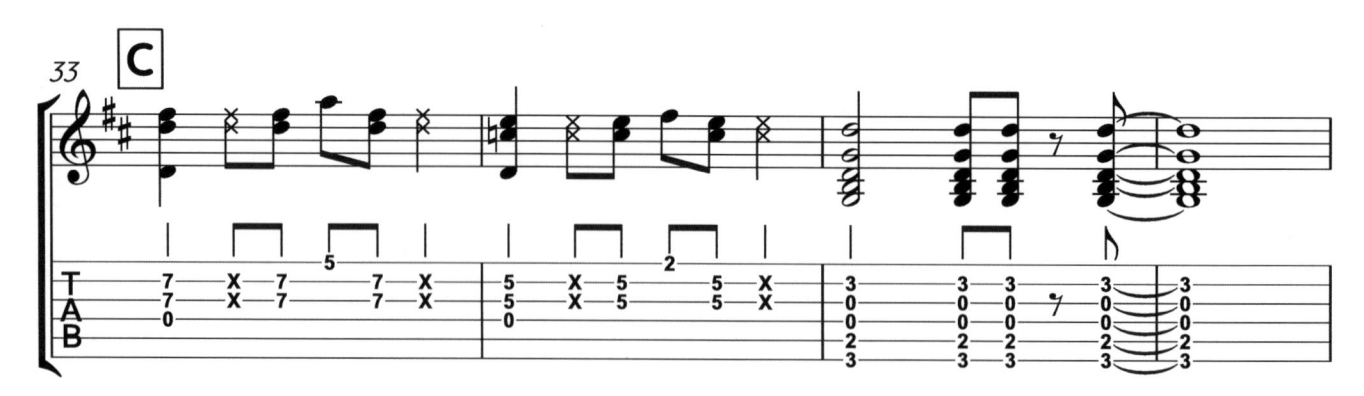

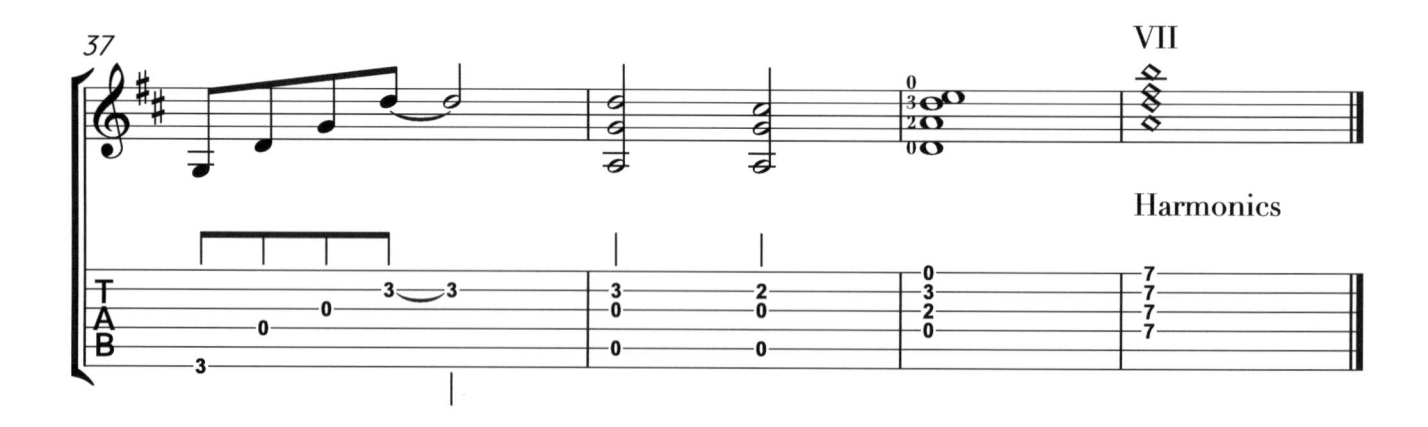

3) Nostalgic - (Grade 3 Level)

Tuning

This may seem an obvious one but being in tune can make the difference between a great performance and a not so great one. This composition has some altered tunings so I'd recommend using a tuner to help you.

When tuning, always tune up from below the note and up to it, this way the string holds its tension and doesn't slip out of tune. I'd recommend always having a tuner attached to your guitar or if you play electro-acoustic or electric. Pedal tuners are also amazingly accurate.

The second focus for this piece is dynamics and touch (being able to keep the hands light whilst playing at varying levels of dynamic). Try to experiment with dynamics, looping a section and playing it *Piano* (Softly) and then *Forte* (Loud or strong).

- Do you press harder with your left hand when you play louder, try to keep the left hand touch as light as possible?
- Do all the notes retain their full and vibrant quality they have when you play loudly and when you play softly?
- Where does the change in attack and volume come from? Your left or right hand?

Changing dynamics on the guitar and keeping both hands relaxed can be a bit like trying to pat your head and rub your tummy at the same time. Like most things on the guitar though if you slow this down and practice the changes in dynamics slowly you will find that soon you have more control of your dynamics and won't feel so tense in your muscles after you finish playing.

A lot of guitarists never work on dynamics, so just being aware of them will give you a head start. Don't forget this applies to electric guitar as well as acoustic, there is a huge amount of dynamic and textural range on the electric guitar without needing to adjust the volume control.

Try study #3 to work on these ideas:

- Play through it only changing the dynamics….from ff to pp
- Now play through it only focusing on the accents, ignore the dynamic markings.
- Now try both, accents and dynamics….tricky hey!
- As before keep the left hand as light as possible when fretting notes. See how little pressure you can use to sound the note.

Dynamics and accents

Study #3

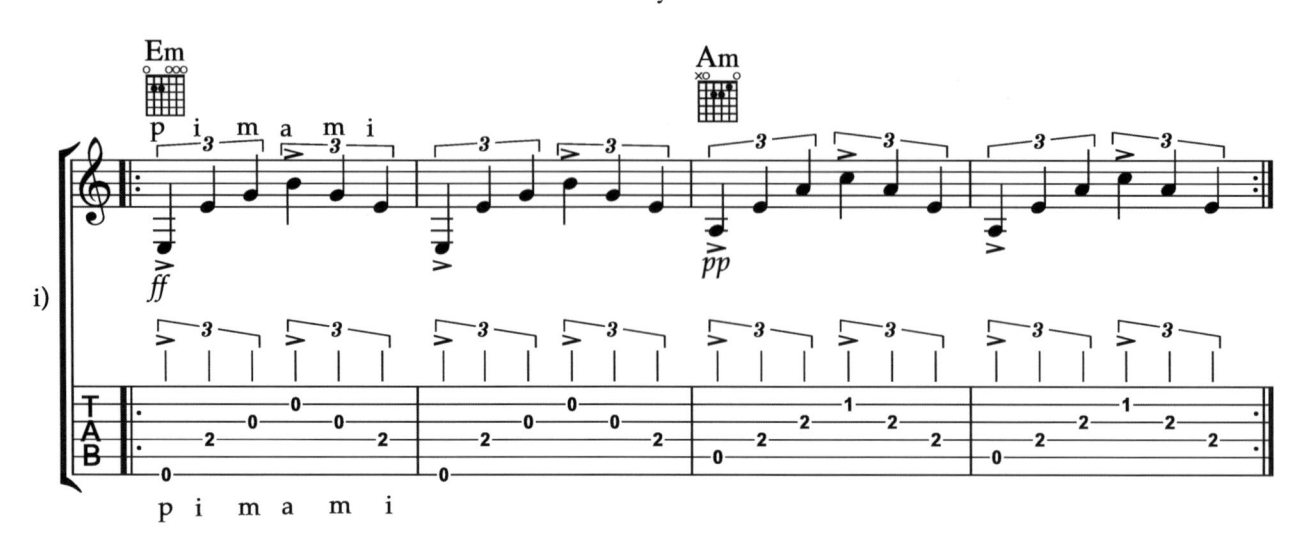

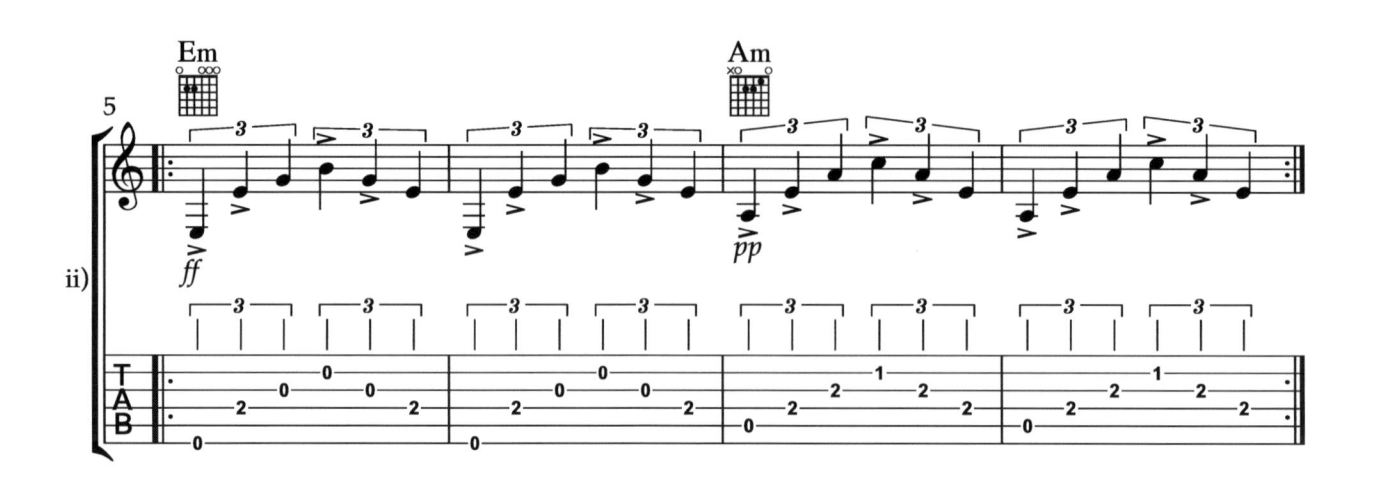

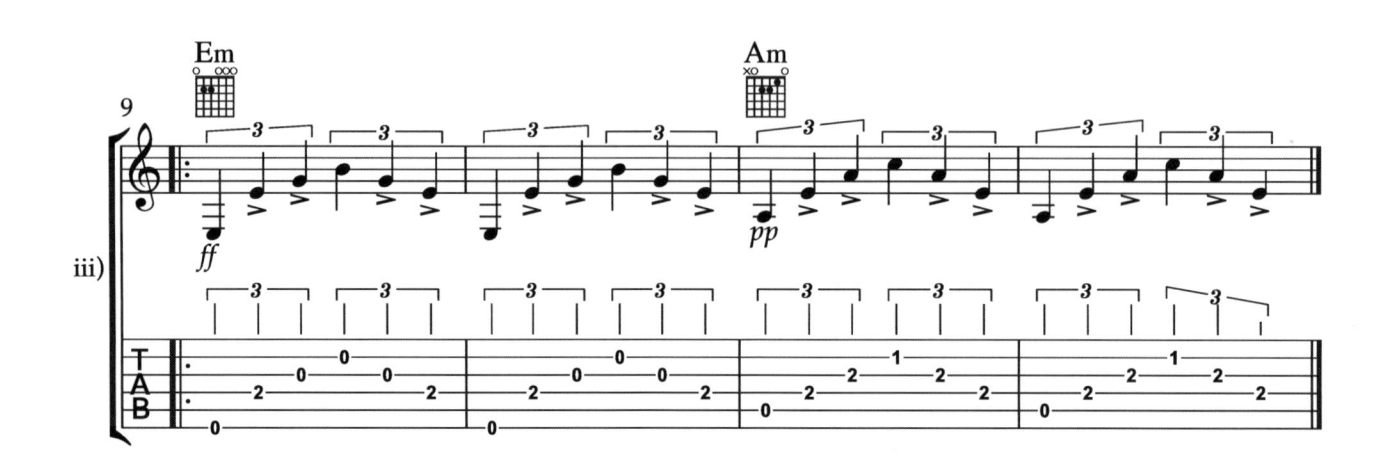

Nostalgic

David Series

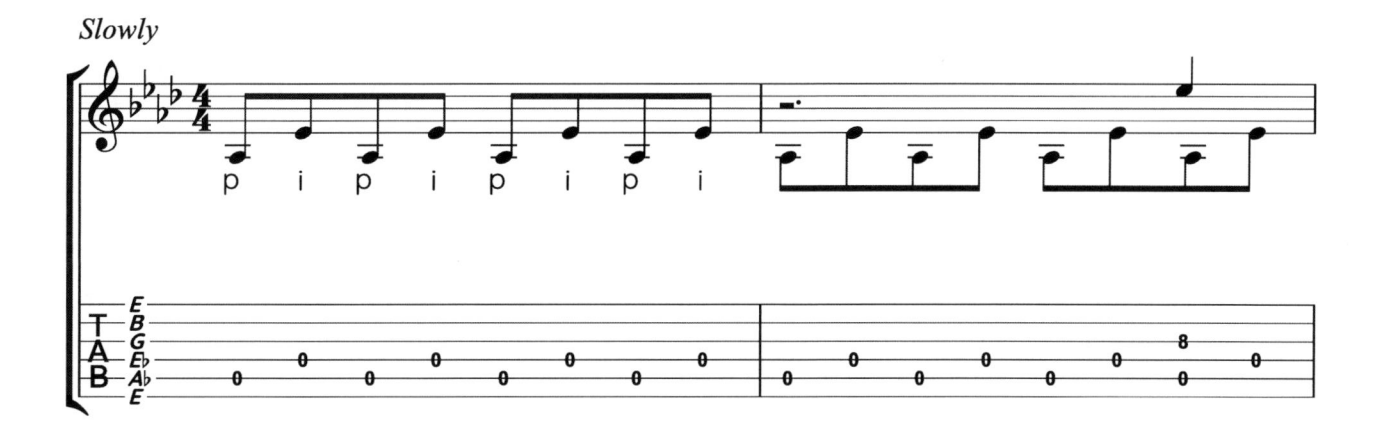

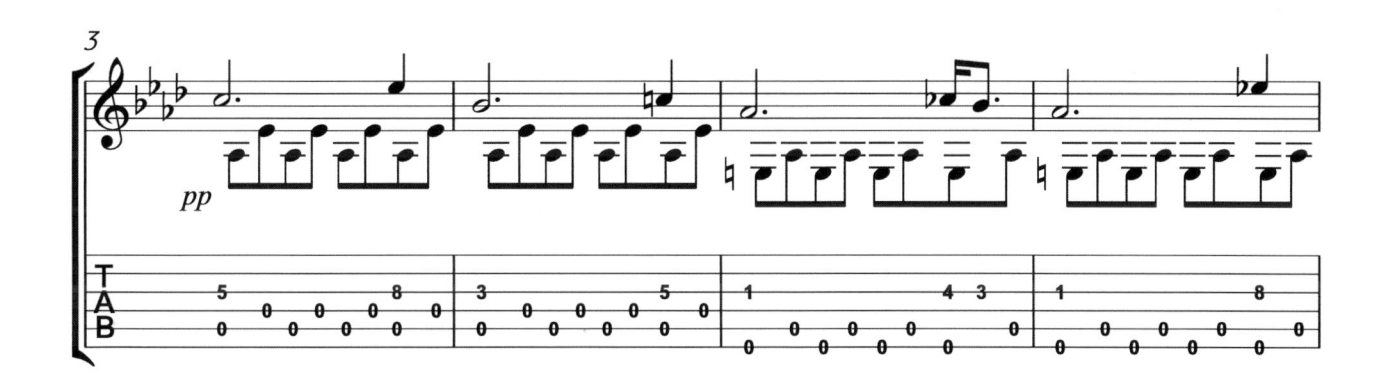

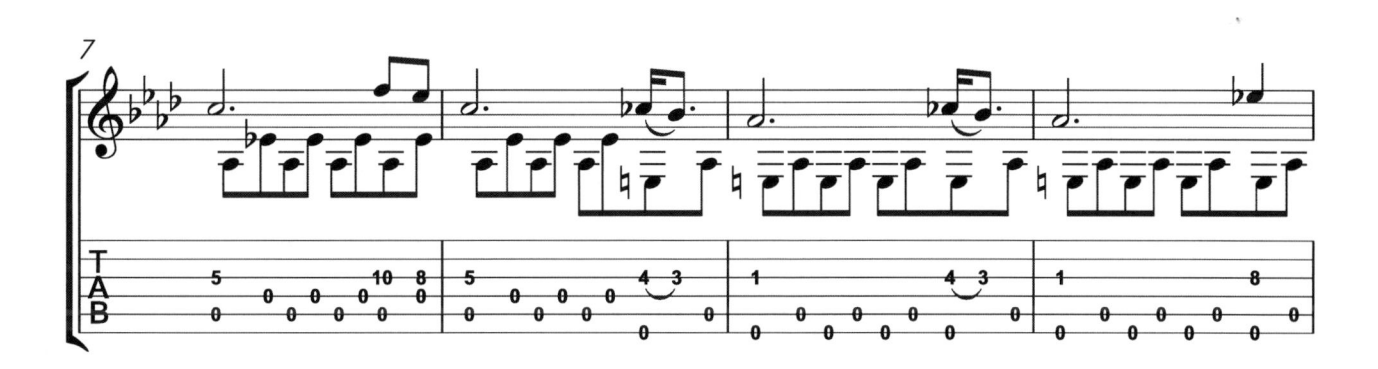

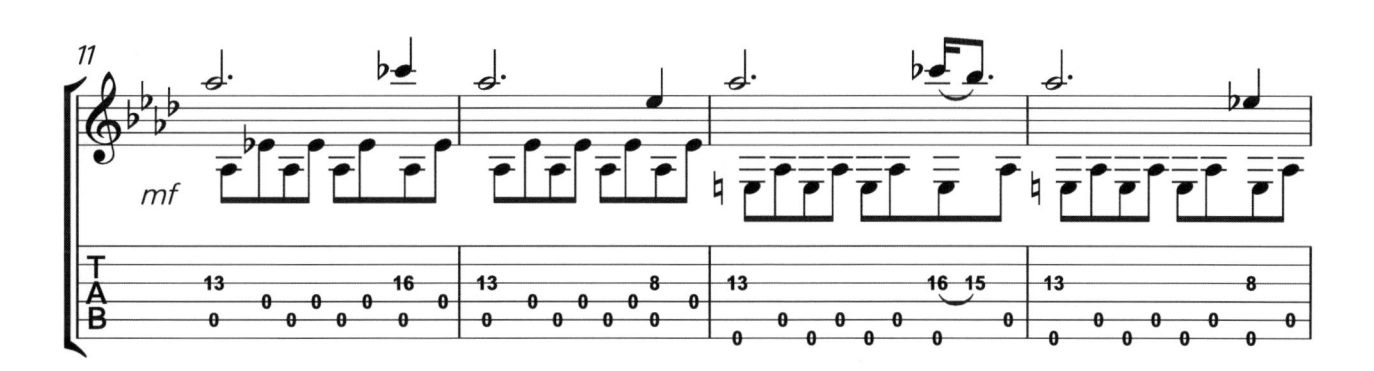

Nostalgic (Continued)

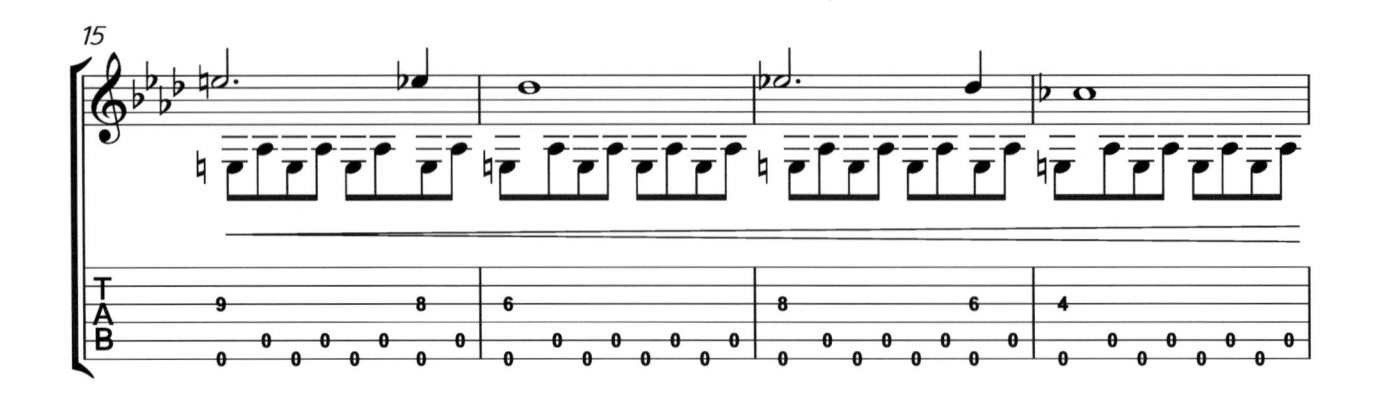

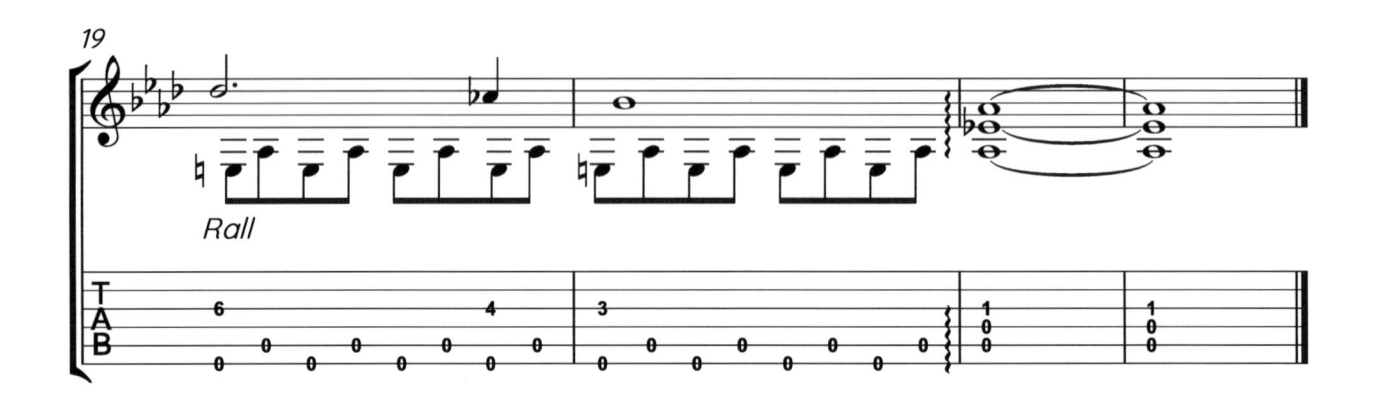

4) Last Embers - (Grade 3/4 Level)
Legato Playing

Legato playing on the guitar is largely down to developing a strong left hand…….. There a various ways to do this though the most obvious is to play through your scales or technical exercises as regularly as possible (five to fifteen minutes a day is great) and focus on legato playing. Study #4 shows an example of how you can work this technique into your playing. There are various finger-strengthening gadgets out there but I've found they just develop painful fingers and wrists. In my opinion it's best to try developing your legato playing with the guitar, practising slowly and mindfully and keeping aware of how relaxed your fingers, arms, shoulders and body are while you go checking in with your breath to make sure you don't hold it in during more tricky to play sections. If the left hand starts to hurt too much…rest…and resume the next day……alternatively you could make your own exercises or compositions focusing on legato playing as a way to integrate it into your playing.

Study #4

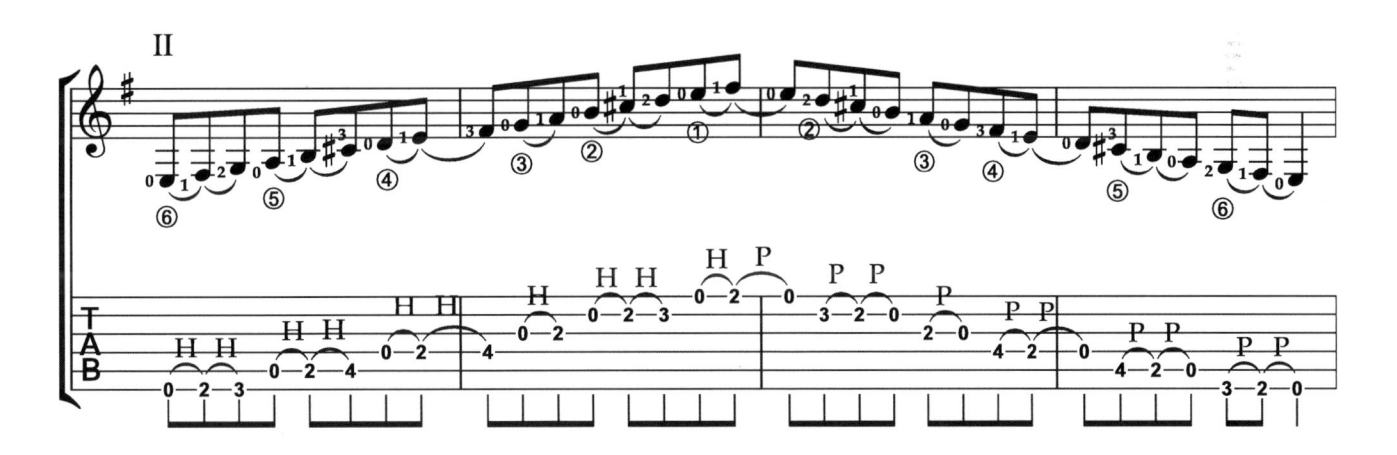

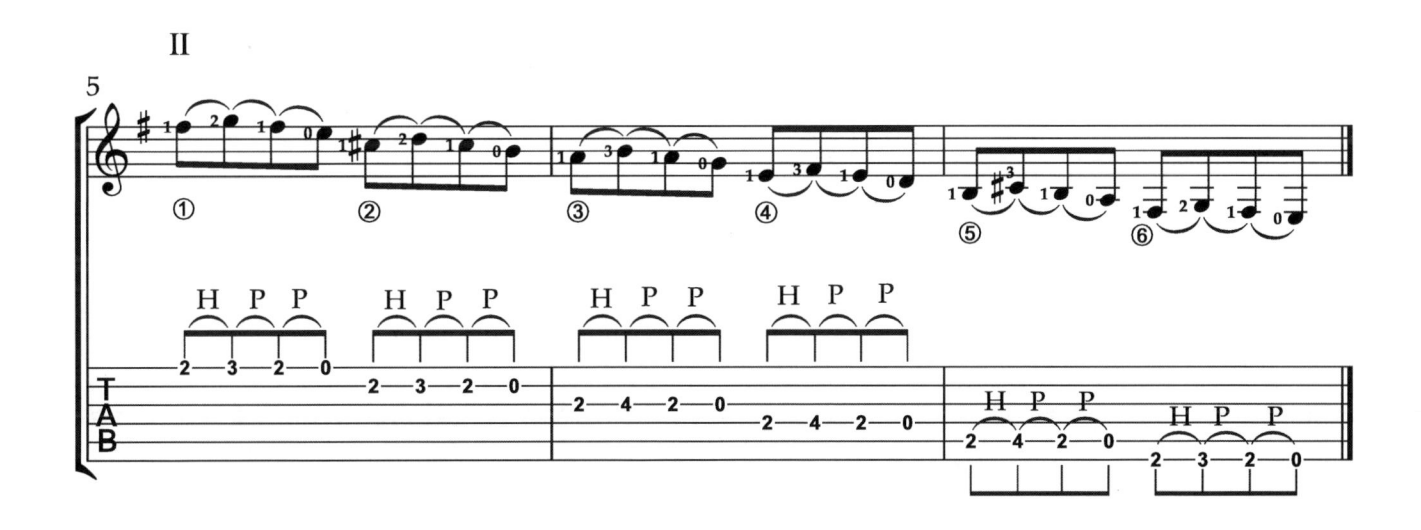

Last Embers

David Series

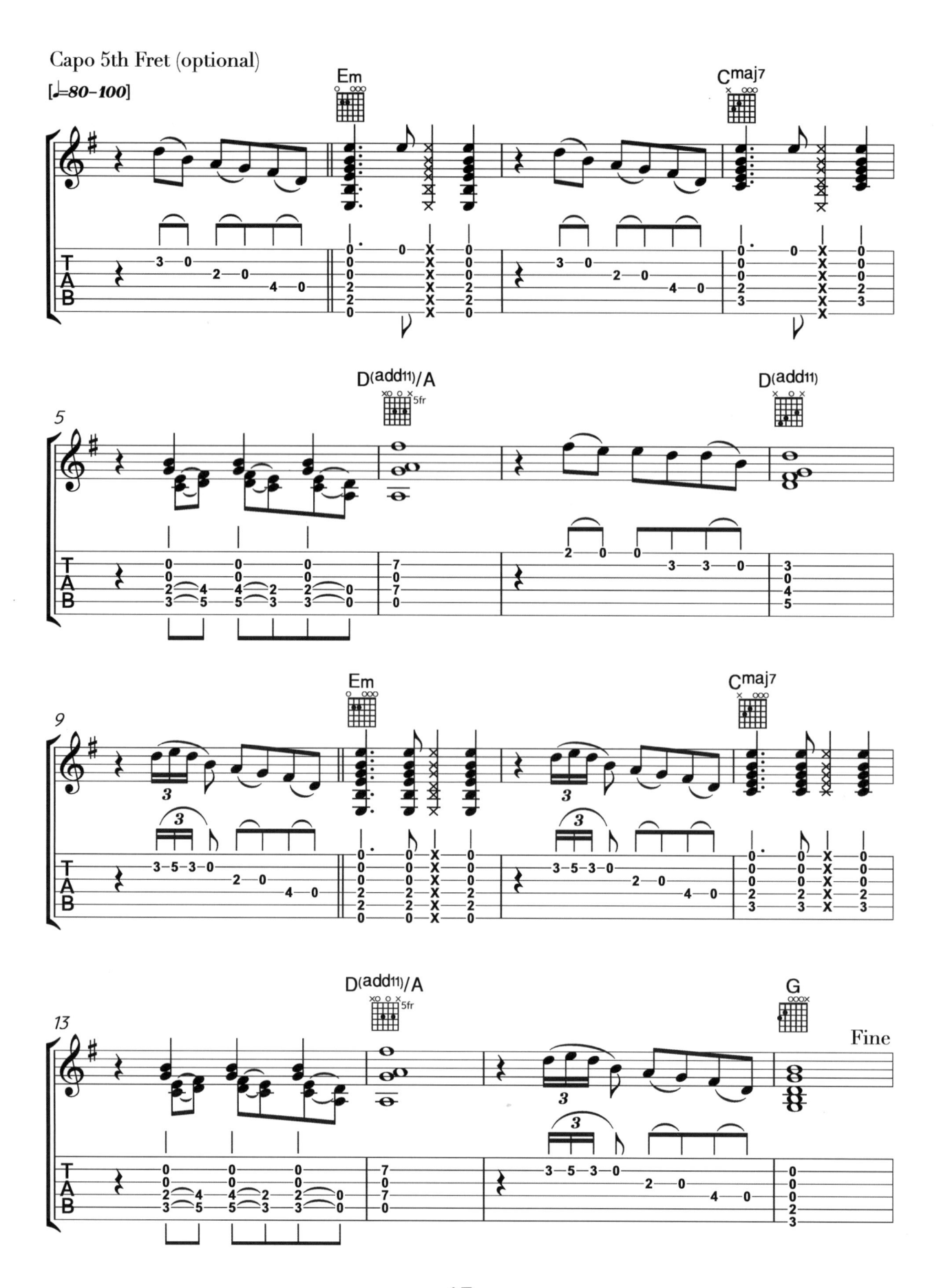

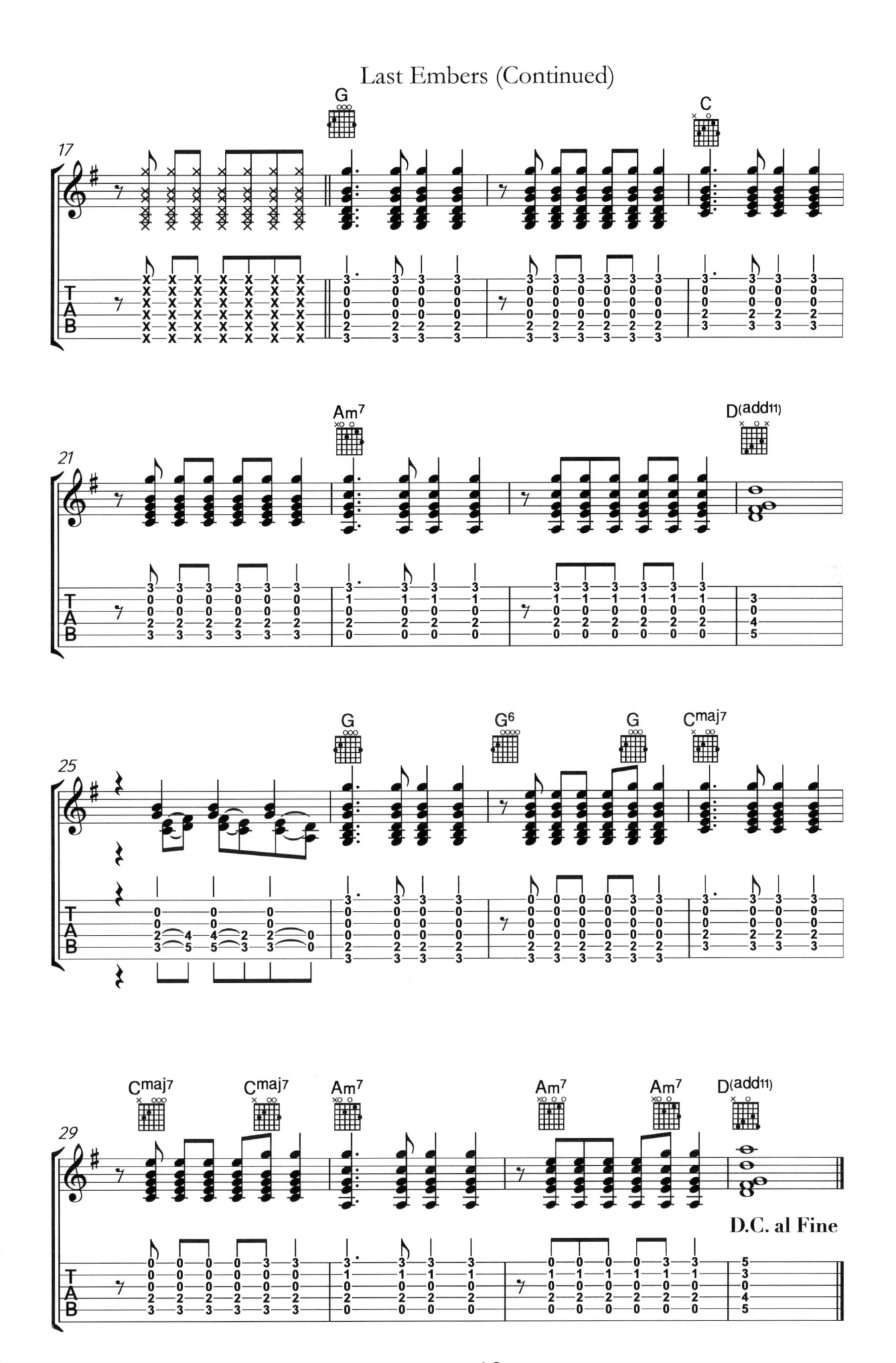

Last Embers (Continued)

Some things to think about....

What music do you listen to?... Do you spend time getting into one album and how much do you try and expose yourself to music away from the mainstream?

Do you record yourself playing regularly?

Do you play with other people, do you want to, how can you get there?

Do you play to other people?

Do you have no desire to play to other people and are perfectly content playing to yourself?!

Have you tried writing your own piece?

How much of the music comes from the guitar itself, how much from you?

What inspires you to play, make a note of these so in times you're struggling for motivation you know what gets you going again!

It is a good habit to keep a practice diary week to week of what you are doing and set small incremental goals.

You can also record your musical thoughts.

Use this space to write any ideas you might have about music, practising, concepts and playing.

(no matter how weird or crazy or ambitious or irrelevant they may seem!)

Remember small goals are good!

5) Aragón (Grade 4 Level)
Major Scale Harmony

Understanding of harmony can really help to open doors in terms of composition, transposing, improvising, general musicianship and being able to communicate your musical ideas to other people. In study#5 we look at how triads and chords are constructed from the major scale and then how they function together in this piece.

Study #5

Chromatic Scale

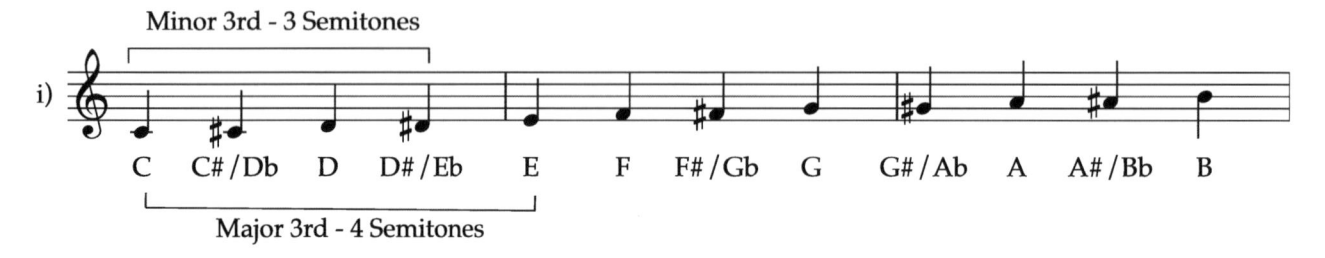

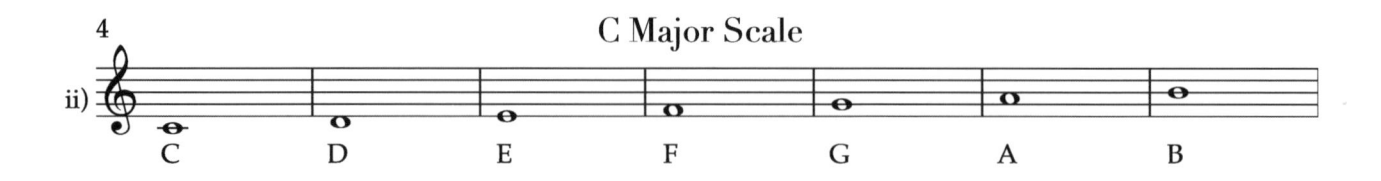

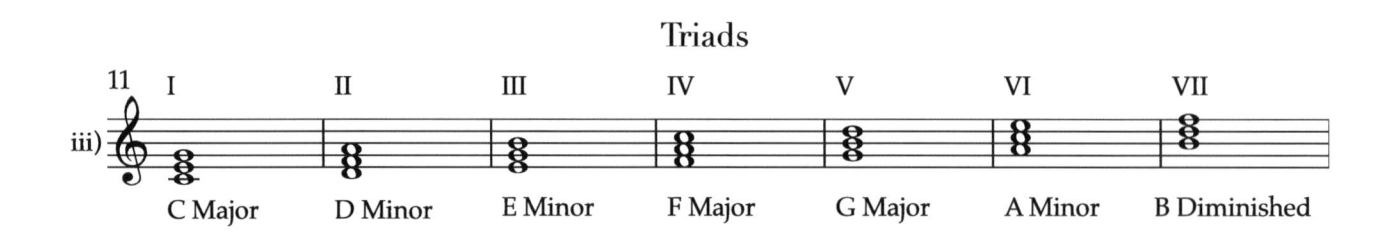

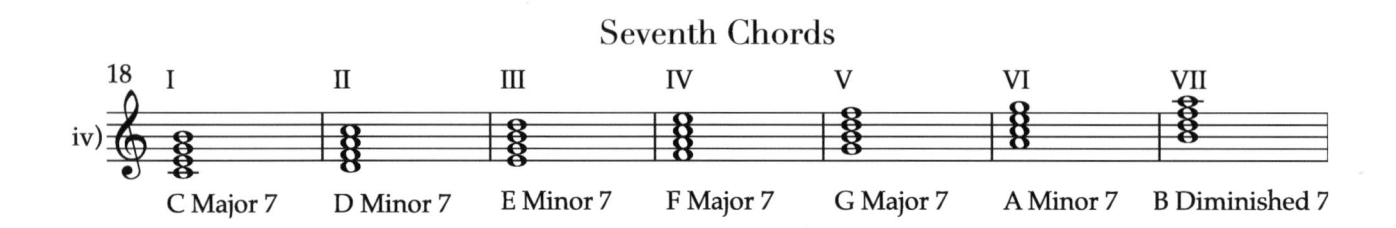

i) C   C#/Db   D   D#/Eb   E   F   F#/Gb   G   G#/Ab   A   A#/Bb   B

Minor 3rd - 3 Semitones
Major 3rd - 4 Semitones

C Major Scale

ii) C   D   E   F   G   A   B

Triads

iii) I - C Major   II - D Minor   III - E Minor   IV - F Major   V - G Major   VI - A Minor   VII - B Diminished

Seventh Chords

iv) I - C Major 7   II - D Minor 7   III - E Minor 7   IV - F Major 7   V - G Major 7   VI - A Minor 7   VII - B Diminished 7

i) Learning the chromatic scale is a really good way of learning the note names. I've left out the TAB or fingerings as I think it's super useful to be able to work out where the notes are for yourself on the fretboard.

When you raise a note by half a step it becomes a sharp(#) and when you lower a note by half a step it becomes a flat(b). On the guitar:

Up/down 1 fret = 1 semitone

Up/down 2 frets = 1 tone

ii) First try to see how many semitones are between each note in the C major scale. So C to D is 2 semitones (C…C#…D). Try working this out on 1 string of the guitar. Starting on the note 'C', first fret of string number 2 (B String).

- Which fret of the second string is D on? Count up…C 1st Fret, C# 2nd Fret, D 3rd Fret.
- Try for the remainder of the notes in the C major scale:

Note	C	D	E	F	G	A	B
Fret (B string)	1	3	?	?	?	?	?

- Which notes of the C Major scale have two semitones between them?
- Which notes have one semitone between them?

iii) **Triads are three notes stacked on top of each other to form a chord.** These are the foundation for most standard harmony. The first triad, C Major, is constructed by taking the root of the scale, (C), and then adding a note that is a Third above the C. So in this case, counting up 3 notes from C we get to E. Then for the next note, count up another third, so you come to the note G. So we get C, E, G. The G is 5 notes up from the C and so called the 5th. In the same we to get the second triad, D minor, we start on the note D…..count up one third, F…..and another third, A. So we get D,F,A, making a D minor chord.

- Which notes do you add on to the note E to make the next chord?
- Try the same for the notes, F, G, A, B
- **Triad chord is Root + 3rd + 5th**

How do you know if it is Minor ot Major?

The way to define a chord as a major or minor chord is by counting the number of semitones between the Root (the bottom chord note) and the third (the next note up in the chord from the root). So…….let's take C major….The root is the note C and the next note up in the chord is an E. There are 4 semitones between the root and the third so this means it is major. If we take the second triad, D minor….the root is D and the third is F….so there are 3 semitones between them…so it is minor. So

Major Chord = 4 Semitones from root to 3rd (Major Third)

Minor Chord = 3 Semitones from root to 3rd (Minor Third)

The diminshed triad: The diminished triad is the odd one out from the major scale…it is two minor thirds stacked on top of each other. So in this case we have B diminished. B - D - F. Between each note there are 3 semitones.

iv) Seventh Chords.

- **To make a seventh chord we take the triad chord (from part iii) and add one more note, a third above, on top of the triad.** So for C major seventh chord we take the C Major triad (C, E, G), and add a B. To work this out count up three notes in the C major scale from the G, arriving at B. So we get C,E,G,B.
- To name the chord correctly we need to count the semitones betwwen the G and the B….so G,G#,A,A#,B…..4 semitones. As looked at in part iii, four semitones is a major seventh. So the chord becomes C major seventh.

- If we jump to the G triad, the fifth triad up we have G major. (G,B,D). Adding the third on to the top of this. Counting up from the D we get to F. So now the full chord is G,B,D,F. We call this G dominant seven. This is because the interval between the D and the F is 3 semitones. (D,D#,E,F)……so a minor third.
- In a similar way, if we take D minor triad (D,F,A), and add the next third on top, we get D,F,A,C. This is D minor seventh. The interval between the top two notes (A,C) is a minor third or 3 semitones.
- So….the three main types of seventh chords are

Major Seventh (Major triad with major third added on top)

Dominant Seventh (Major triad with minor third on top)

Minor Seventh (Minor triad with minor third added on top)

- The odd one out is the chord built on the note B. In this case called B half-Diminished. It is a diminished triad with a major third added on top (F to A…4 semitones).
- Seventh chord is Root + 3rd + 5th + 7th

A lot to think about! Don't worry you don't need to know all this before you play, it's just good to try and slowly understand how the notes and chords are all related bit by bit as you go along. Slowly it will start to make sense the more you question things.

QUIZ

1)   How many semitones between these notes:

C and D _____

E and F _____

G and A _____

D and F _____

F and A _____

Which of the above are minor or major triads?

2) Name these chords :

E,G,B,D _____

F,A,C,E _____

G,B,D,F _____

A,C,E,G _____

3) How many semitones make up a minor third? _____

4) How many semitones make up a major triad? _____

5) What is the interval between the G and the B string on the guitar, major or minor third? (count the semitones from G to B)

FINALLY….**You can see the chords are all numbered, I, II, III, IV, V, VI, VII. This is really important in learning music and try to memorise these as much as possible whilst growing as a musician.**

Aragon

David Series

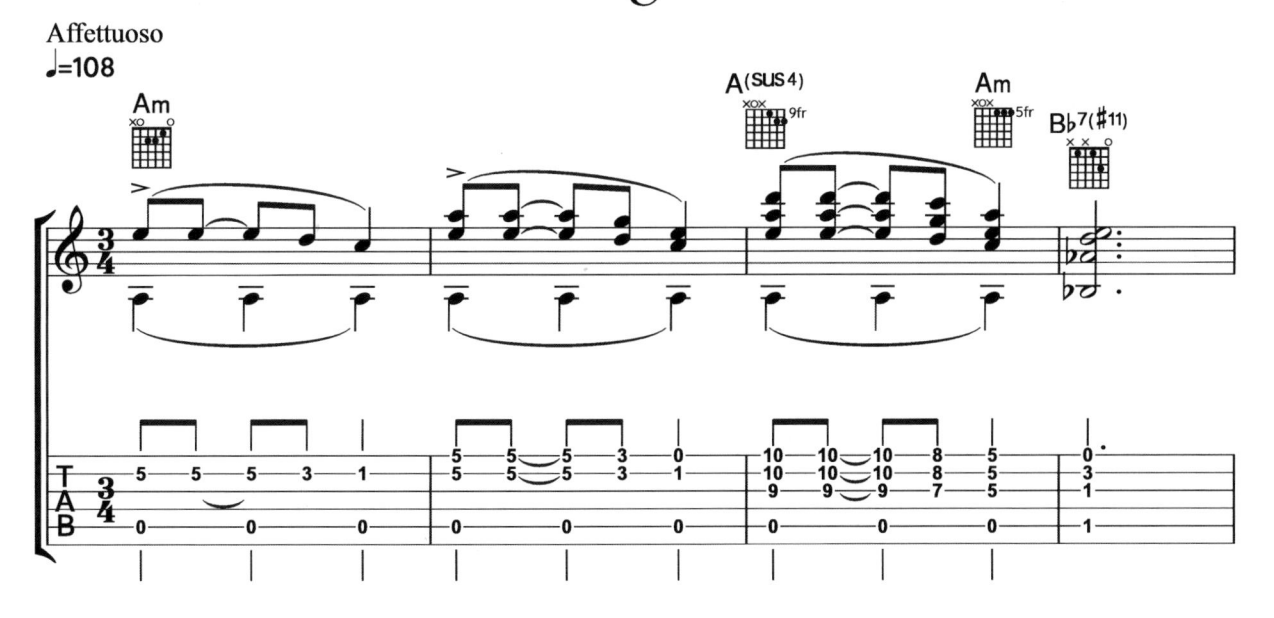

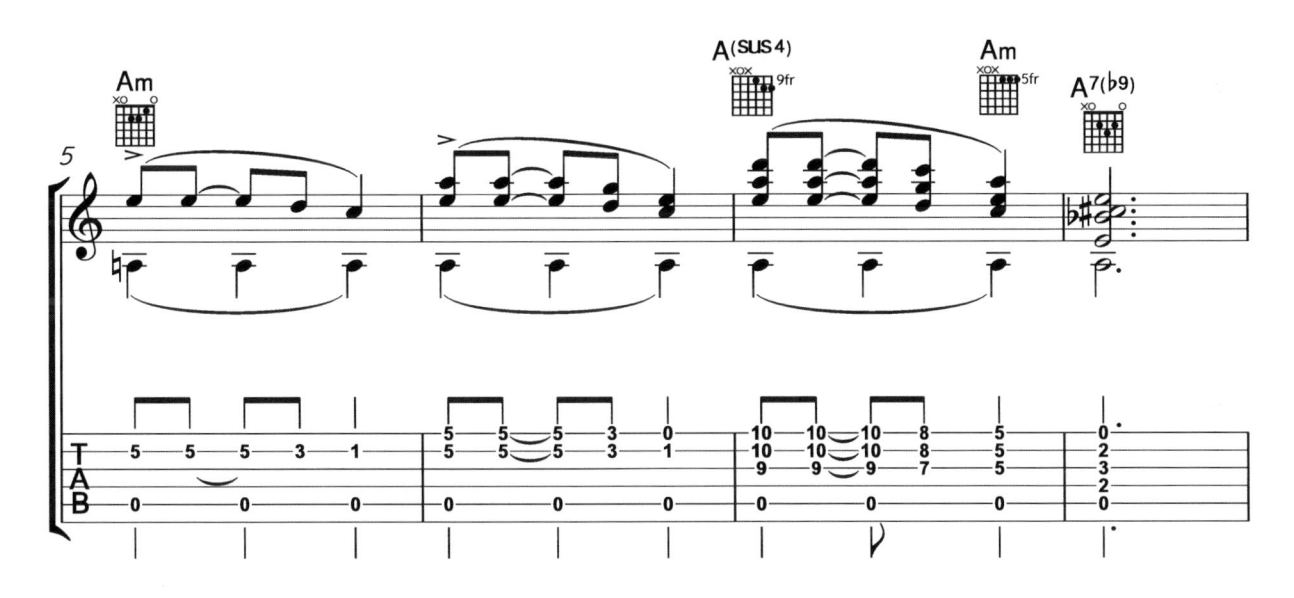

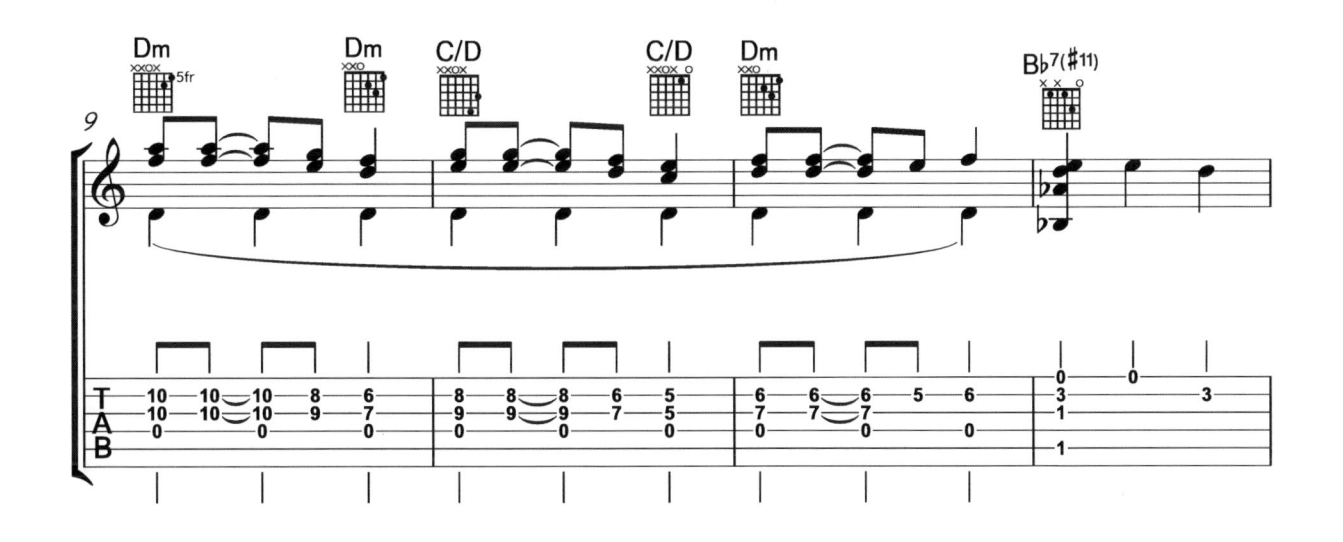

Aragon (P2)

Aragon (P3)

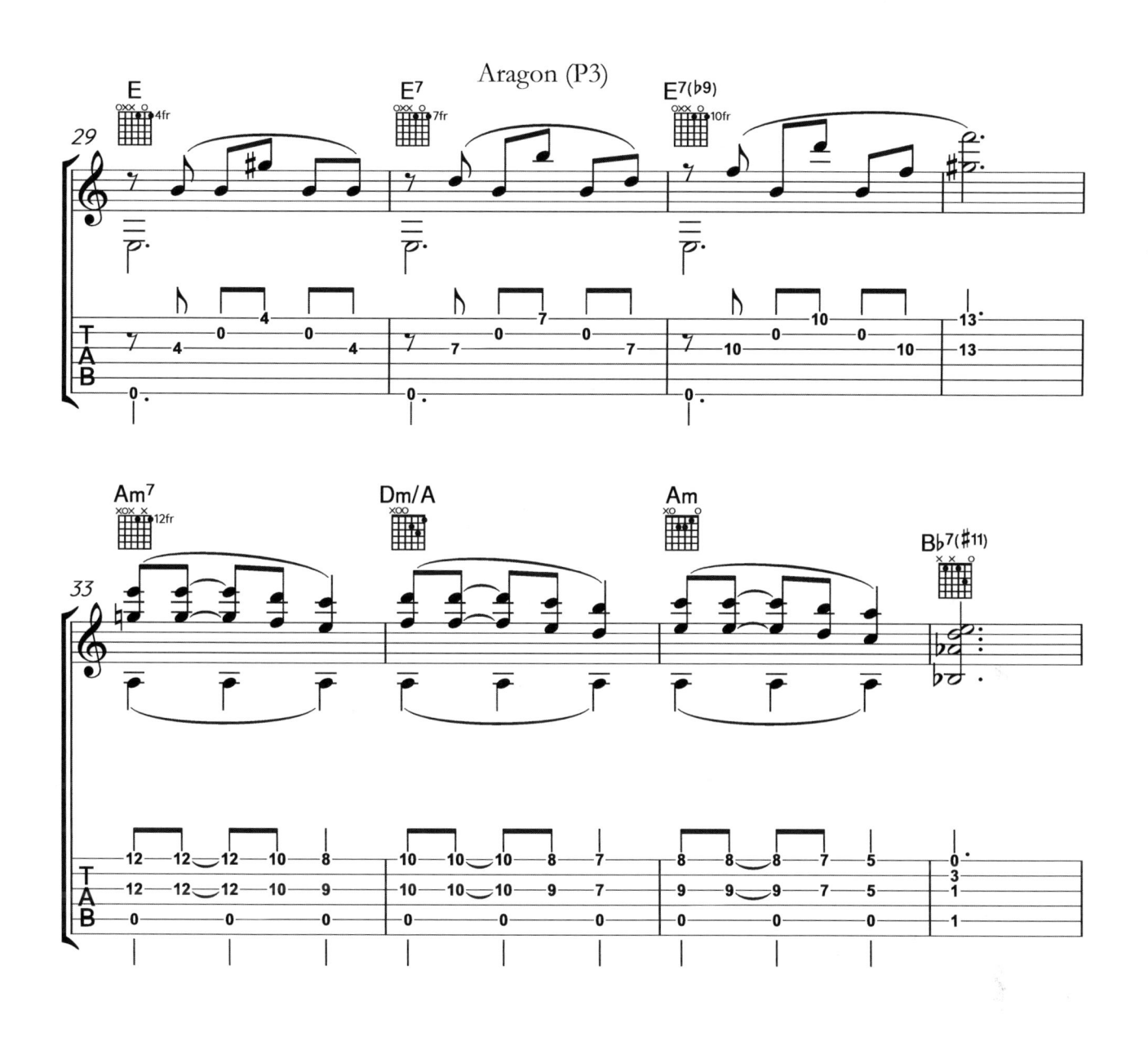

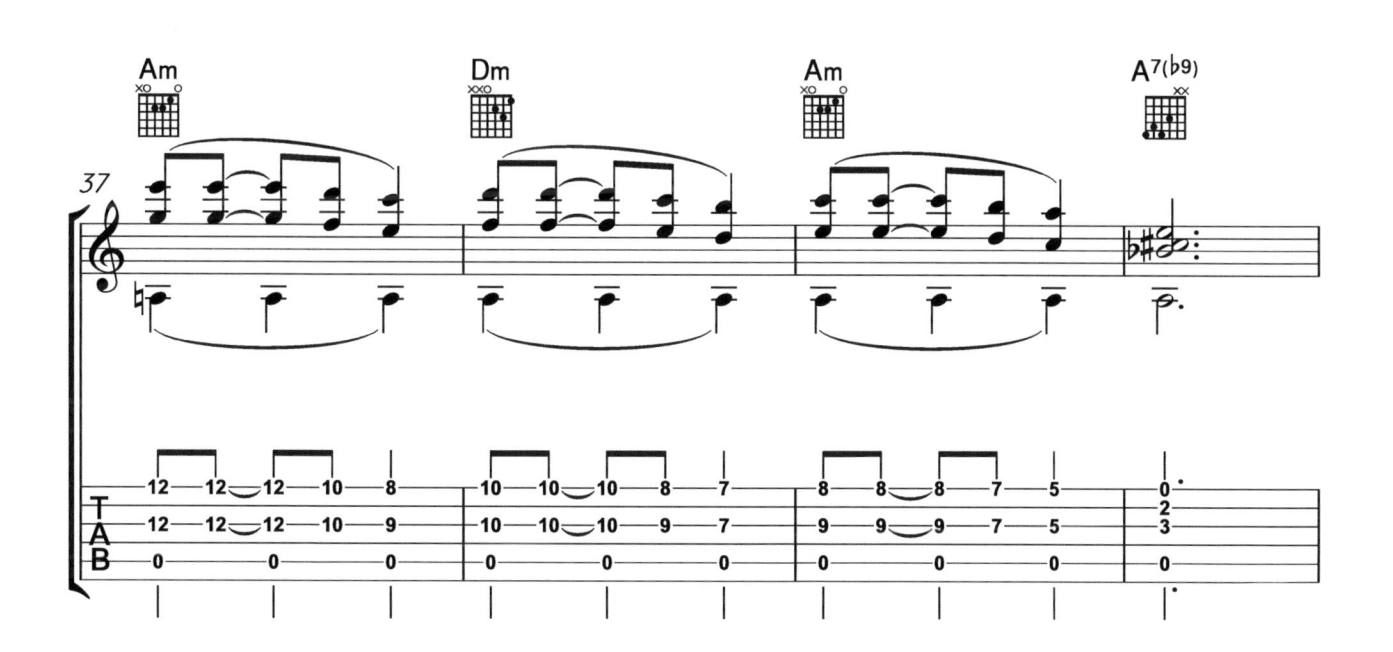

Aragon (P4)

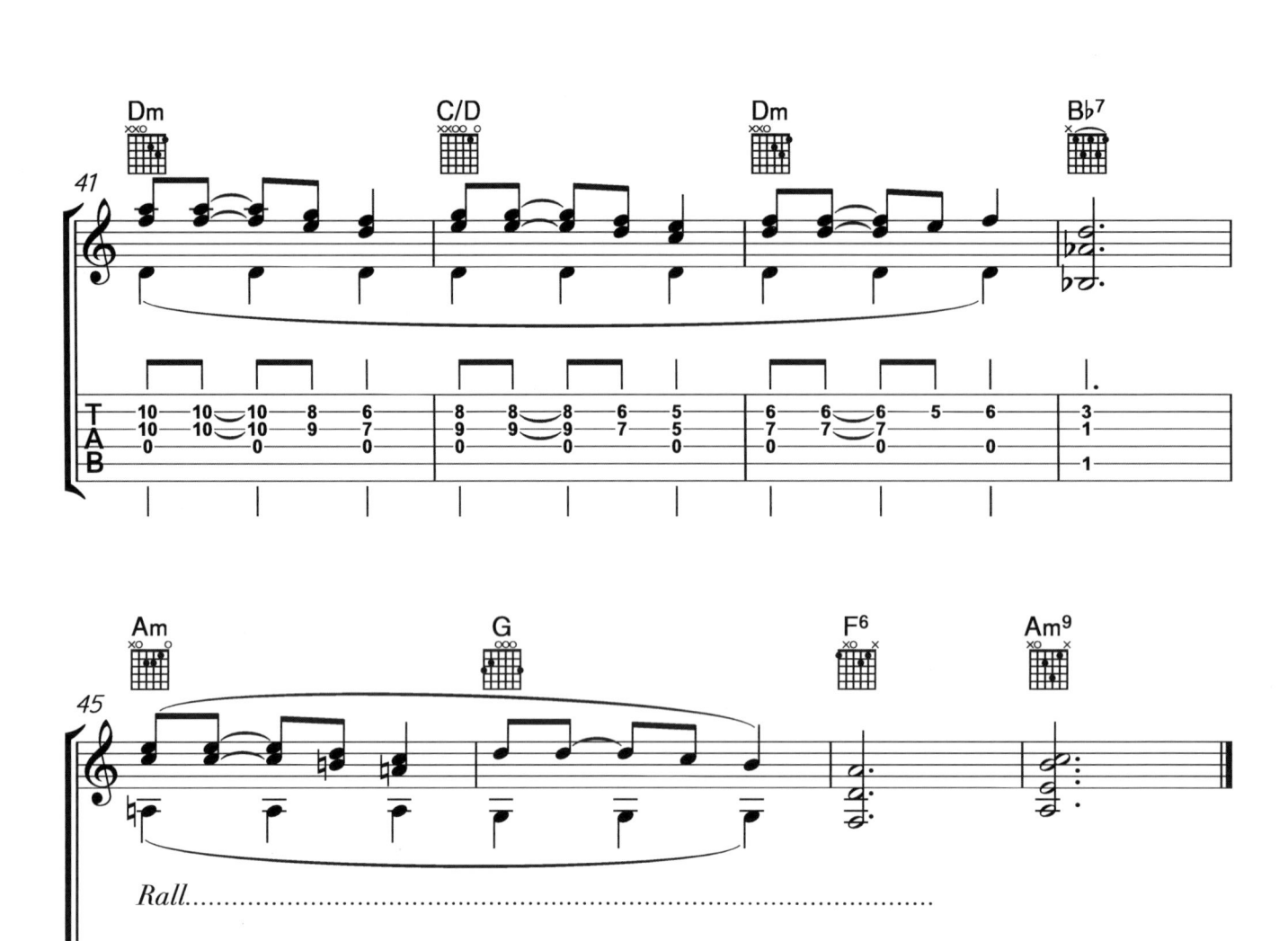

Before we go on to the next piece…………..let's look at some of the chords from Aragón……C Major 7, A minor, D minor and G7.

- Can you give the chords in the piece numbers??* (from the roman numeral system)…..remember C major scale builds these chords:

	I	II	III	IV	V	VI	VII
Triads.	C major	D minor	E minor	F major	G major	A minor	B diminished
7th Chords.	C Major 7	D minor 7	E minor 7	F major 7	G dominant. 7	A minor 7	B half-diminished 7
Symbol.	CMaj7	DMin7	EMin7	FMaj7.	G7	Amin7	B min7b5
Alternate symbol	CΔ7	D-7	E-7	FΔ7		A-7	Bø

(*You might notice that the notes in the piece are sometimes stacked up in a different order e.g. instead of C,E,G it maybe C,G,E…fear not…these are called inversions of the chords. It's important to first study them in their simplest form and then later we can move on to looking at inversions of chords).

6) Bongo Bobi - (Grade 4 Level)
Rhythmic accuracy and subdivisions

I've found teaching in schools and even whilst studying in colleges in the UK that the rhythmical side of music is often neglected. I was lucky enough to study for a short time in Spain, there they have a huge emphasis on rhythm. This piece is a good one for working on your rhythmic accuracy and feel.

Study#6

This study is about getting used to feeling each part of the bar......... The idea is you say out loud Ta-ka-di-mi Ta-ka-di-mi and then clap the rhythms notated. Why have I not written it as 1 + 2 + 3 + 4 +??!, and chosen to use konnakal??(A rhythmic system from Northern India)............... Well, I find it a lot less tiring saying Ta-ka-di-mi, Ta-ka-di-mi, Ta-ka-di-mi, Ta-ka-di-mi for a minute or so rather than 1 + 2 + 3 + 4 +, 1 + 2 + 3 + 4 +,1 + 2 + 3 + 4 +. I find students respond in the same way. It is also an introduction to an amazing rhtyhmic tradition that is thousands of years old that is far more advanced than anything that has been developed in the Western world. So why not? I guess it's useful to know both, but for practical purposes in this study we will explore rhtyhm with konnokal.

- Work your way through these quaver rhythms (8th notes), trying to keep the Ta-Ka-Di-Mi count flowing throughout.

Study #6

This time a similar idea with semiquavers (16th Notes)

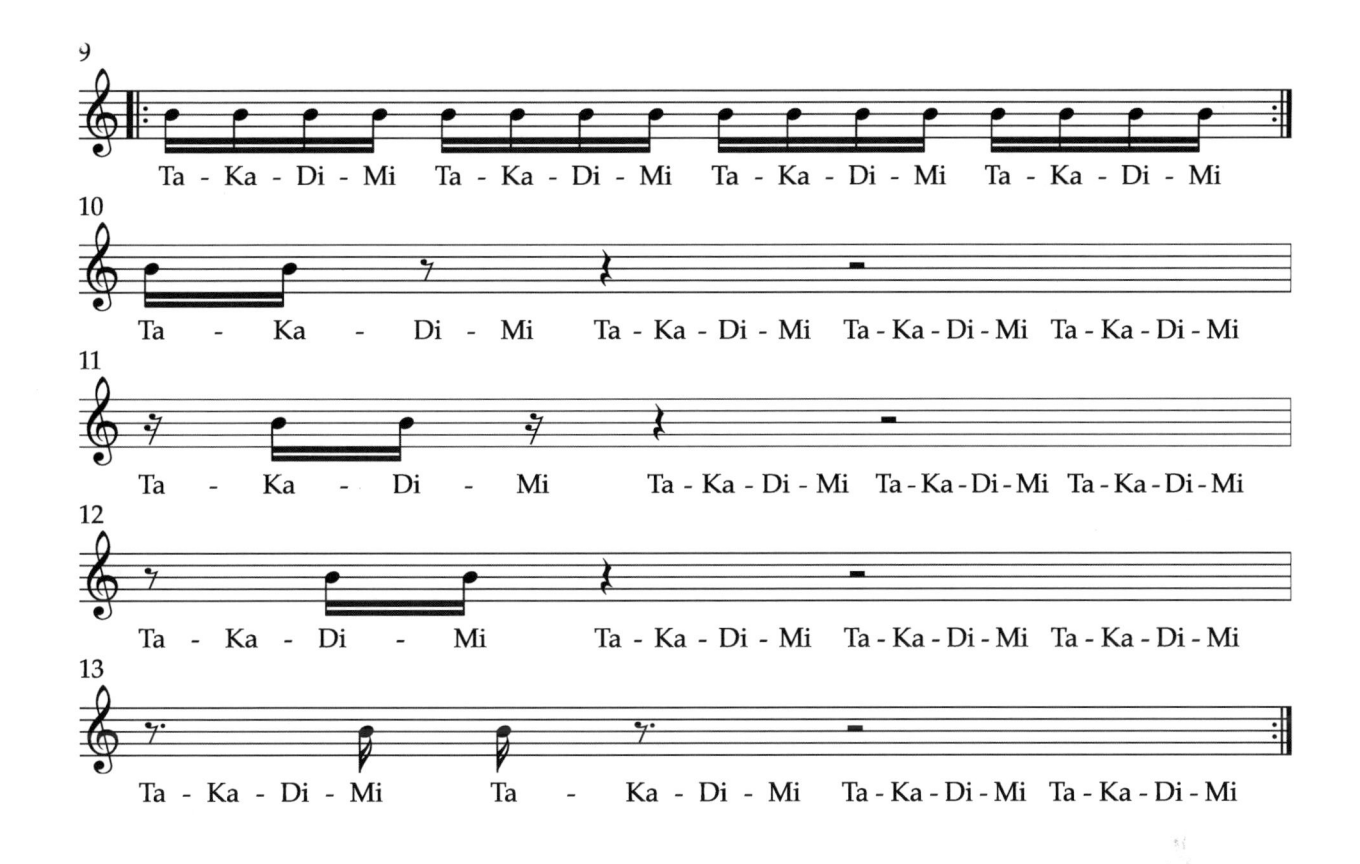

9
Ta - Ka - Di - Mi   Ta - Ka - Di - Mi   Ta - Ka - Di - Mi   Ta - Ka - Di - Mi

10
Ta - Ka - Di - Mi   Ta - Ka - Di - Mi   Ta - Ka - Di - Mi   Ta - Ka - Di - Mi

11
Ta - Ka - Di - Mi   Ta - Ka - Di - Mi   Ta - Ka - Di - Mi   Ta - Ka - Di - Mi

12
Ta - Ka - Di - Mi   Ta - Ka - Di - Mi   Ta - Ka - Di - Mi   Ta - Ka - Di - Mi

13
Ta - Ka - Di - Mi   Ta - Ka - Di - Mi   Ta - Ka - Di - Mi   Ta - Ka - Di - Mi

Now try the same with the main rhythm from Bongo Bobi

14
Ta - Ka - Di - Mi   Ta - Ka - Di - Mi   Ta - Ka - Di - Mi   Ta - Ka - Di - Mi

Once you've got the hang of these try doing the same thing but instead of clapping the rhythms play them on the guitar using whatever chord or note you like.

Optional: Put paper on the bridge to make percussive sound (Weave through strings)

Bongo Bobi

David Series

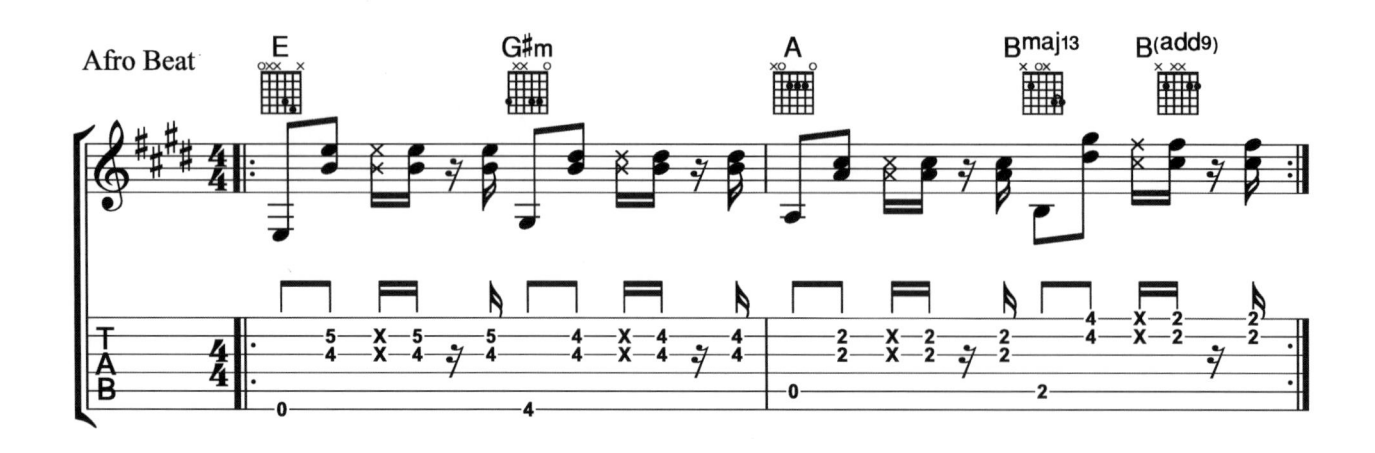

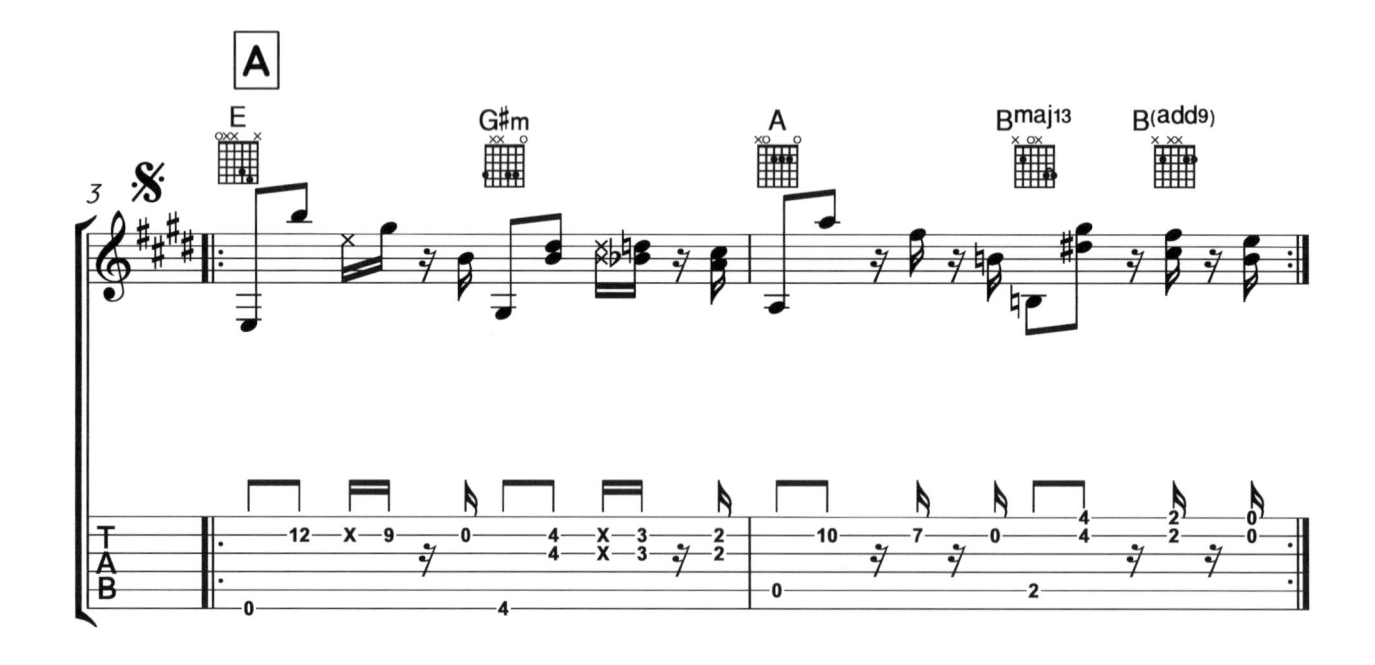

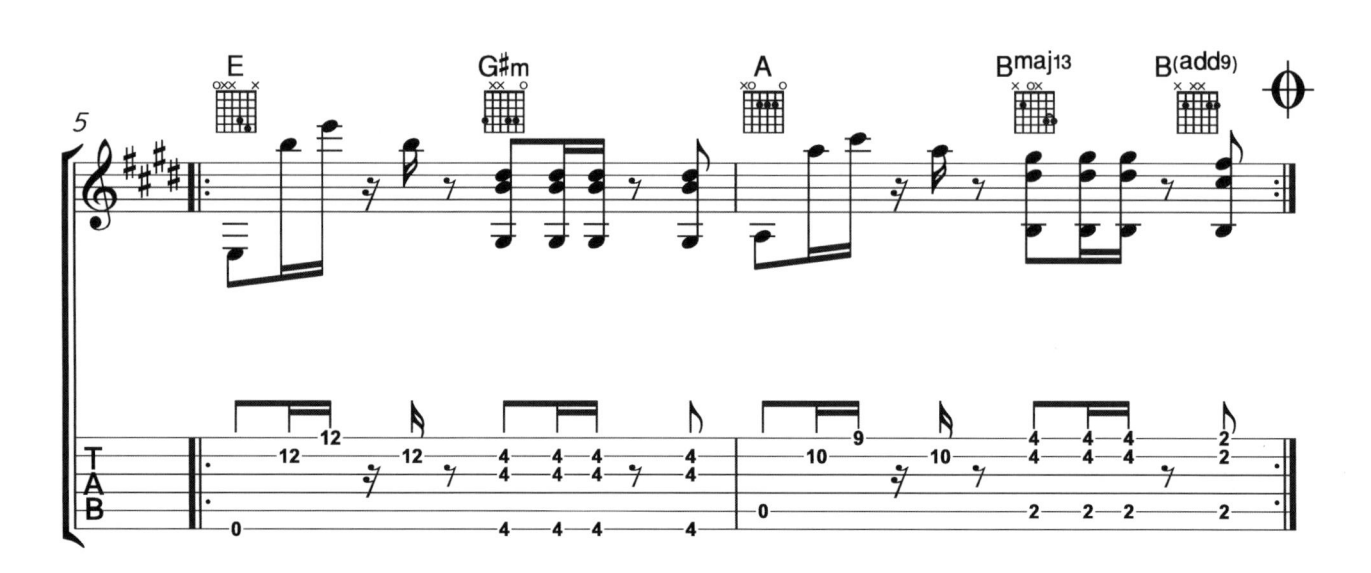

Afro Beat

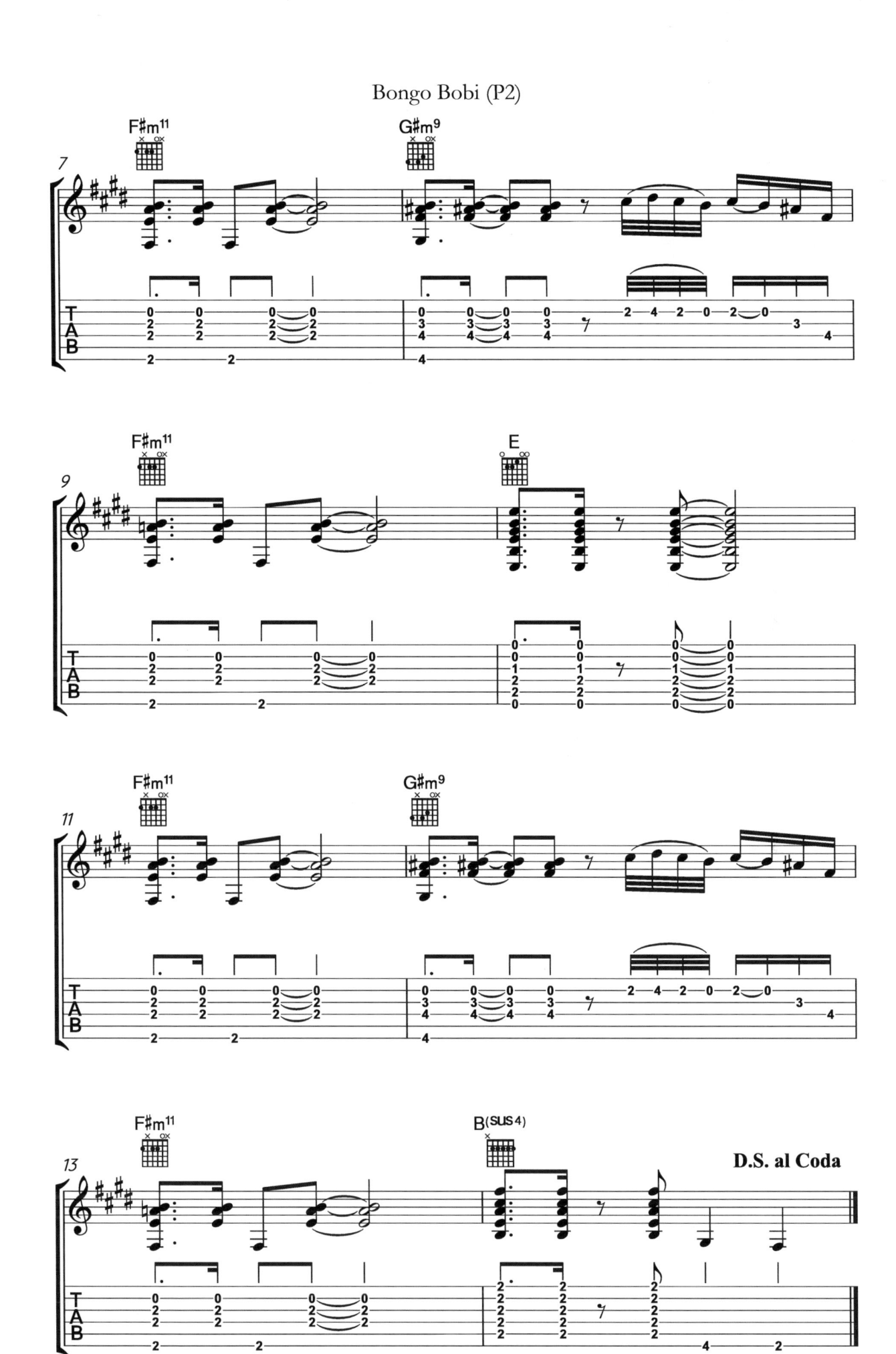

Bongo Bobi (P2)

Bongo Bobi (P3)

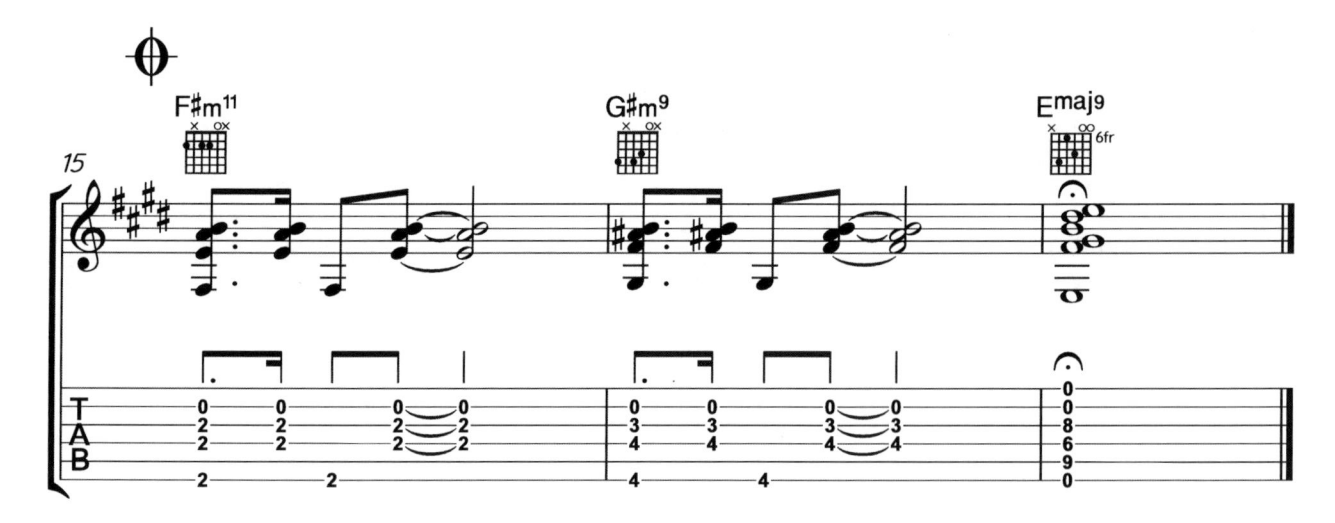

7) Glow - (Grade 3/4 Level)
Chordal playing technique

This time I wanted to look at learning to play chords clearly i.e. with each string ringing without being muted unintentionally. Often, especially to start with, on the guitar, it is hard to get your left-hand fingers around all the notes so as to have them all sounding clearly. In study#7 and this piece there are plenty of opportunities to have deadened strings sounding, maybe having been accidentally muted with the left hand. So the challenge this time is to make all the notes that you intend to play sound clearly....it can be harder than you think! Don't worry if it doesn't happen straight away, just being aware of it through trying these exercises will allow it will mean your playing will become clearer over time.

Study#7

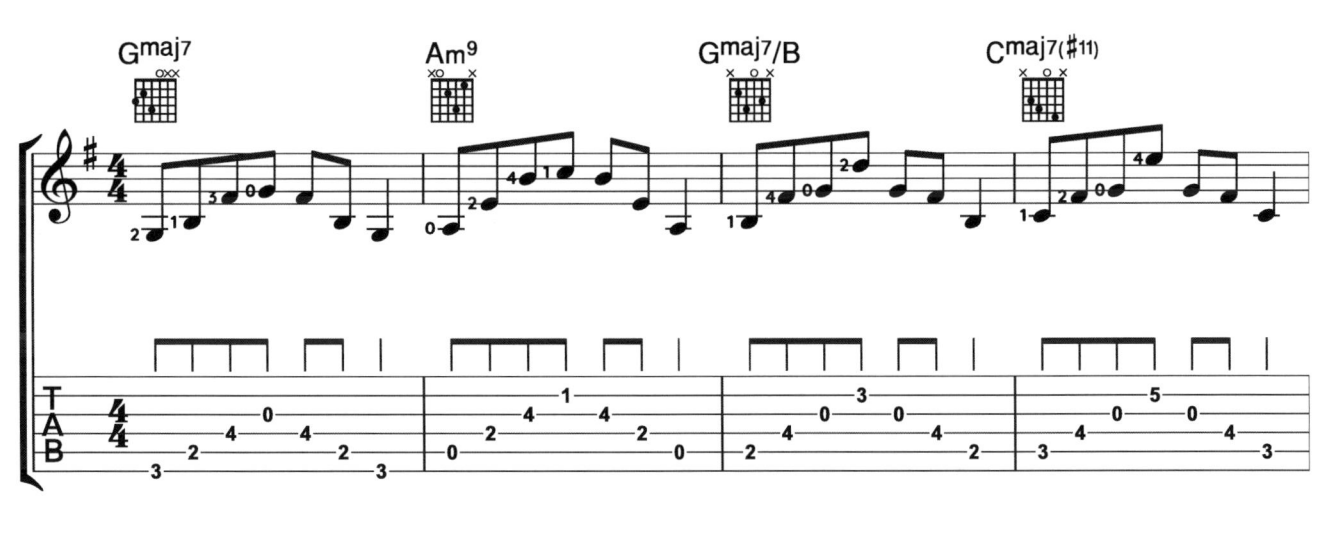

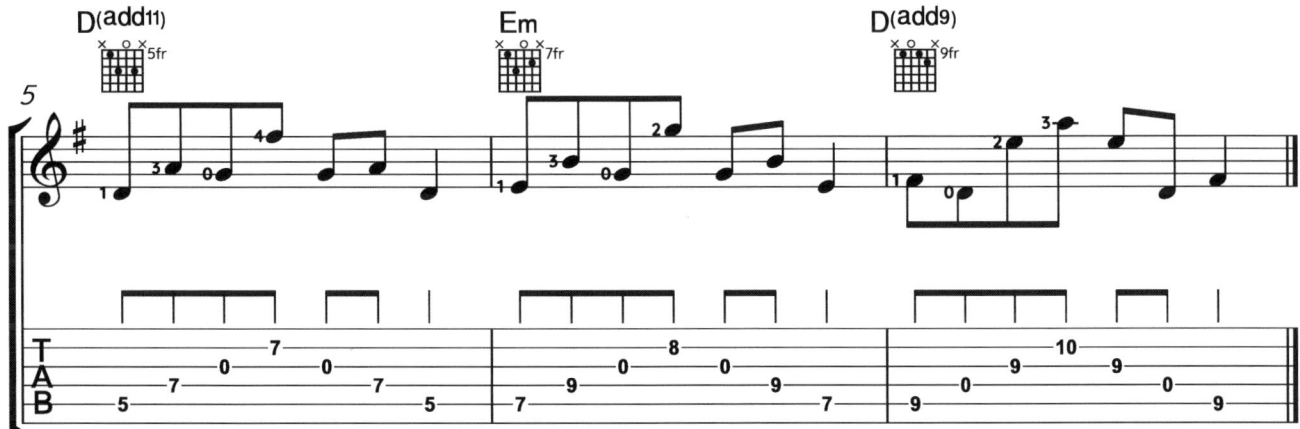

Glow

David Series

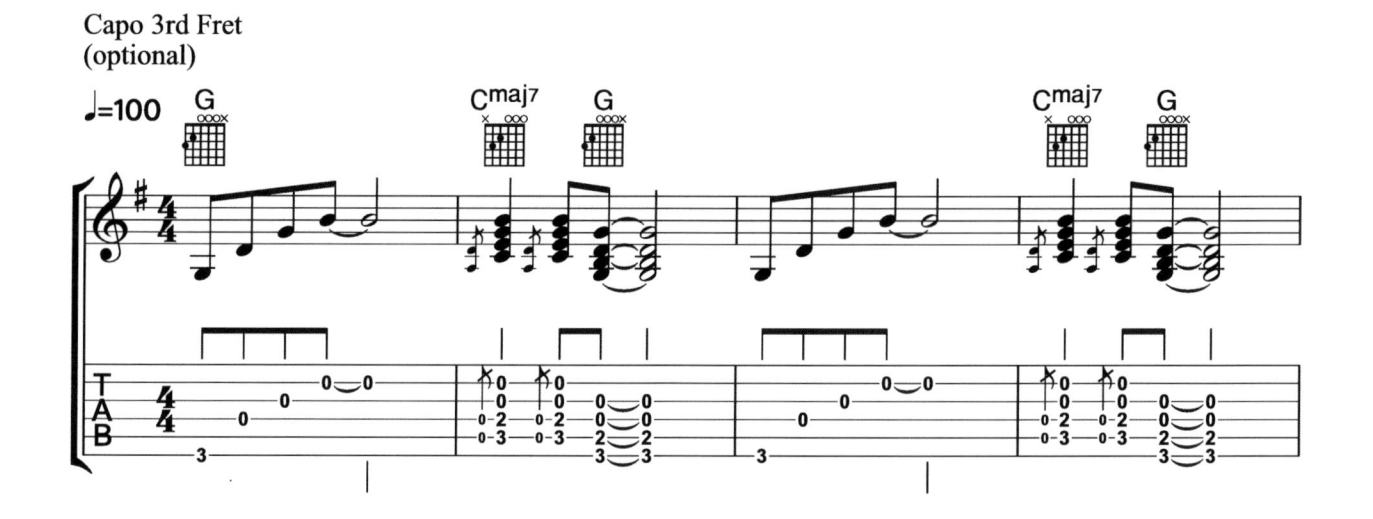

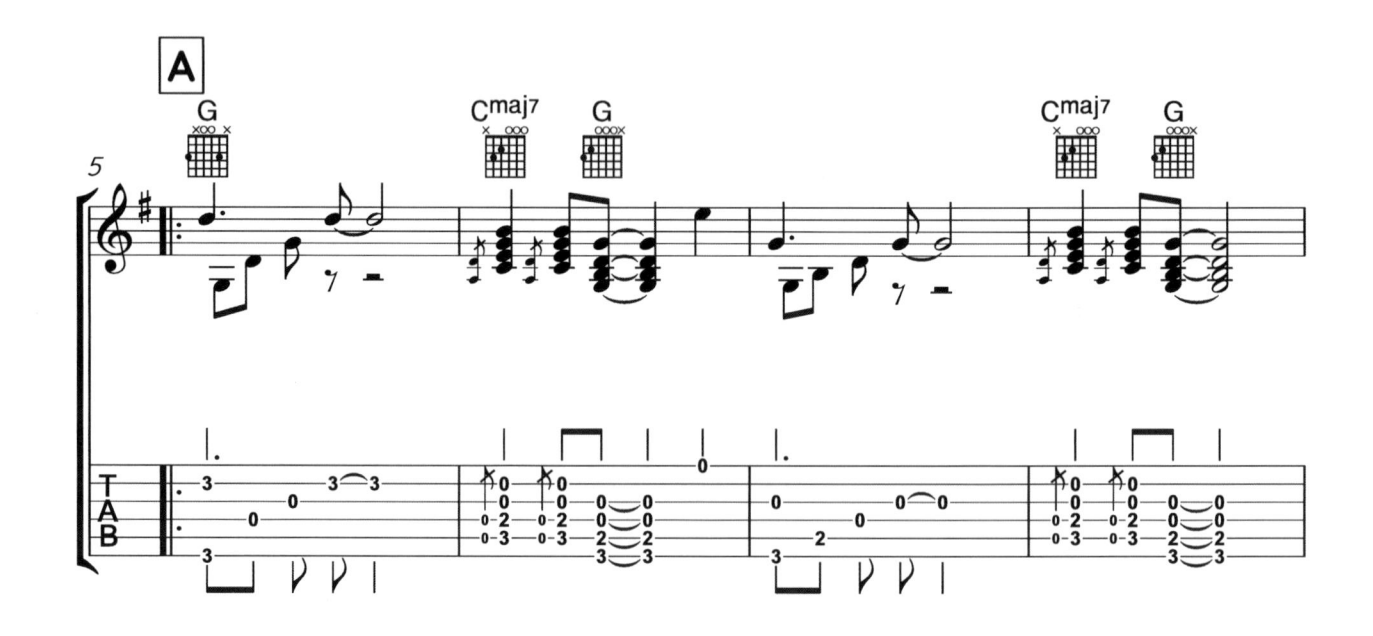

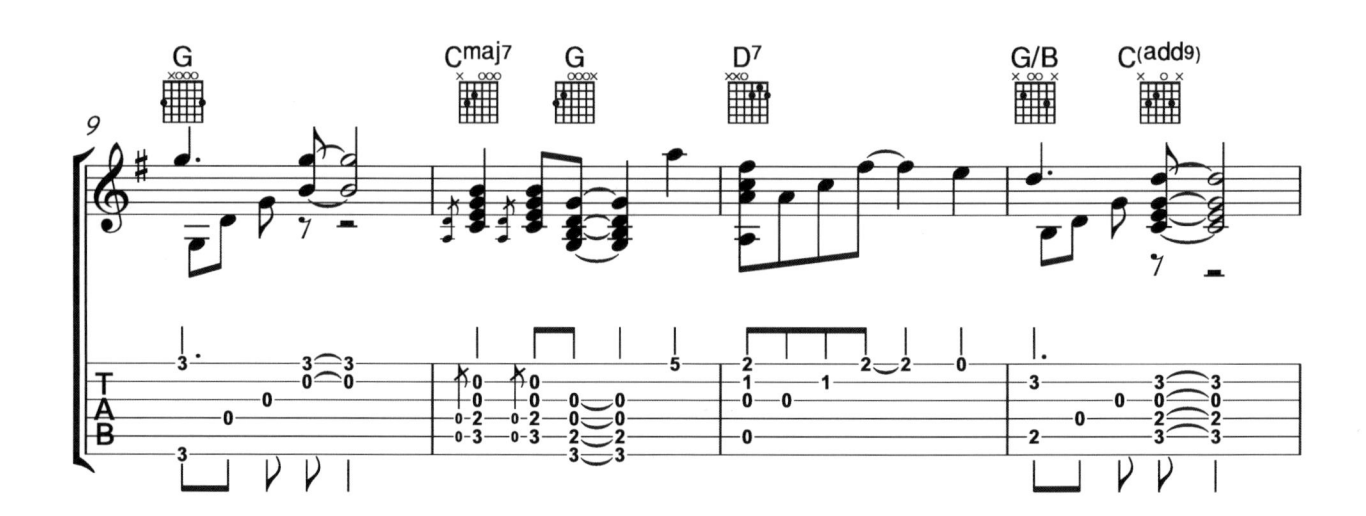

Capo 3rd Fret
(optional)

♩=100

Glow (P2)

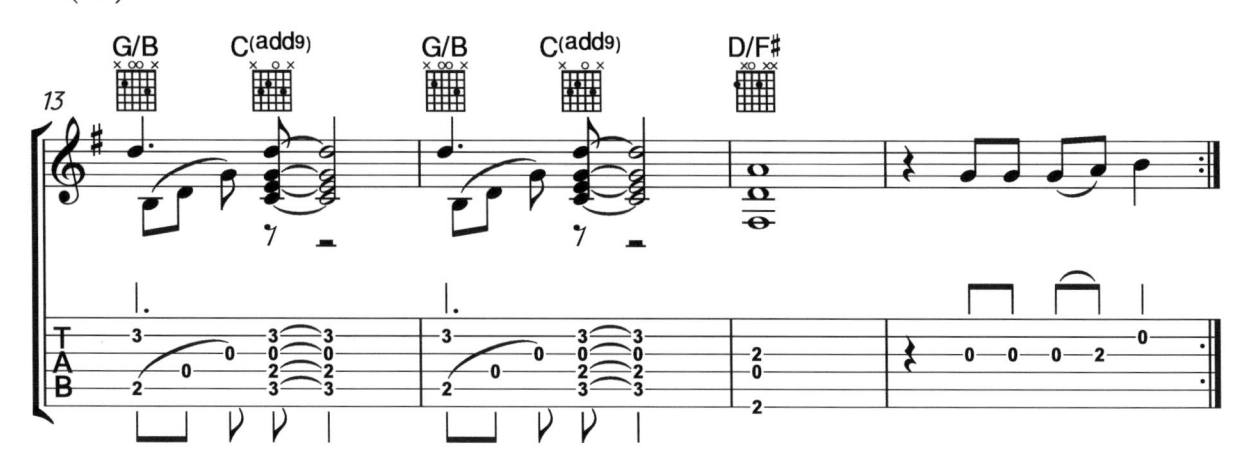

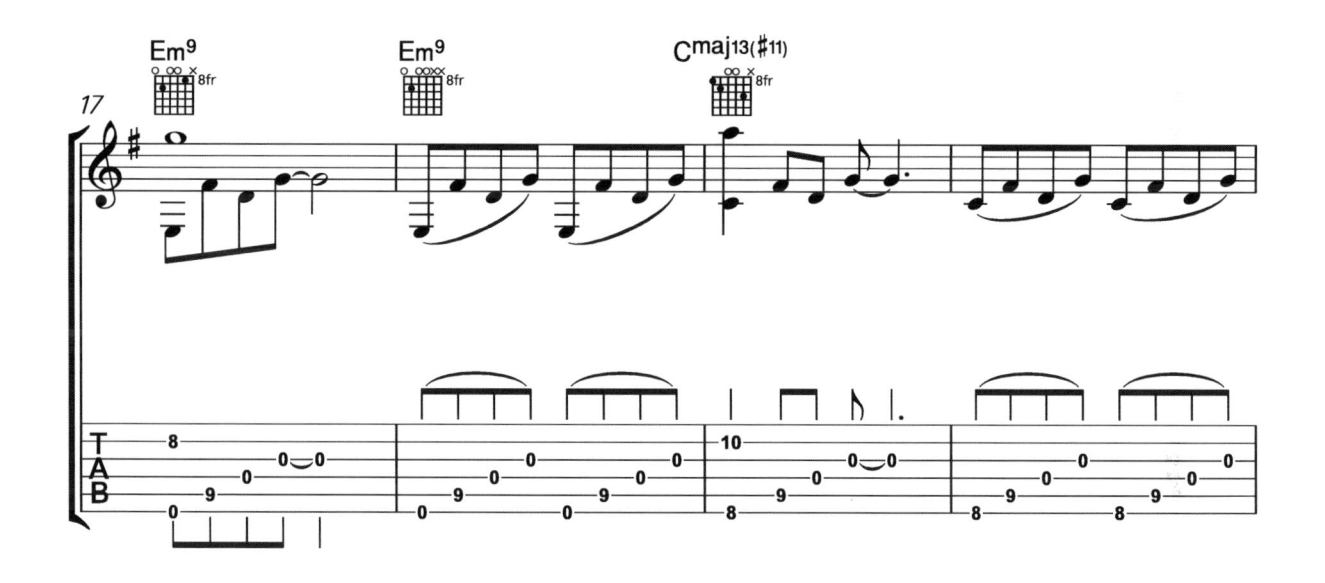

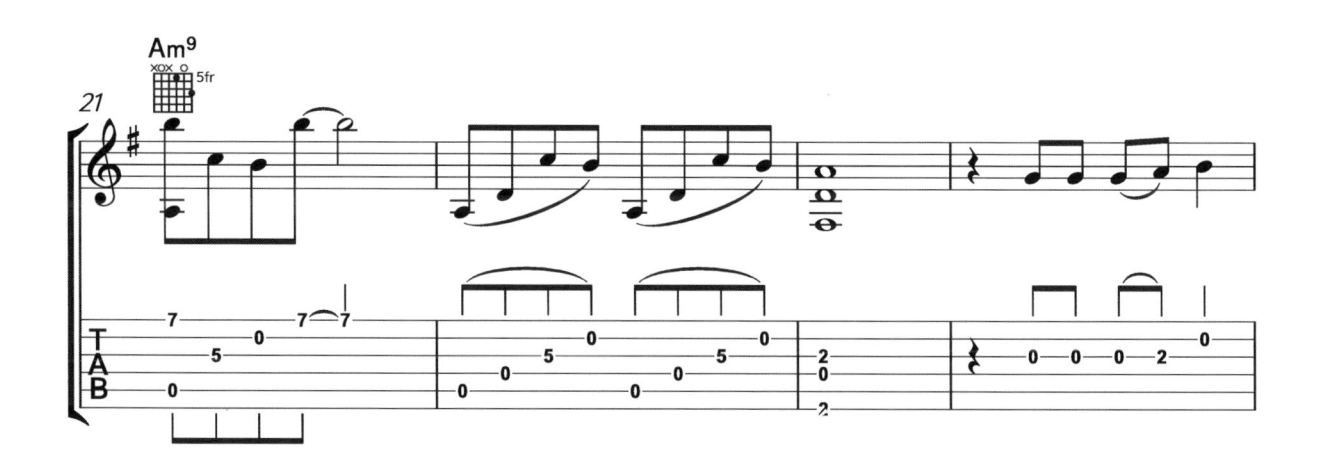

Glow(P3)

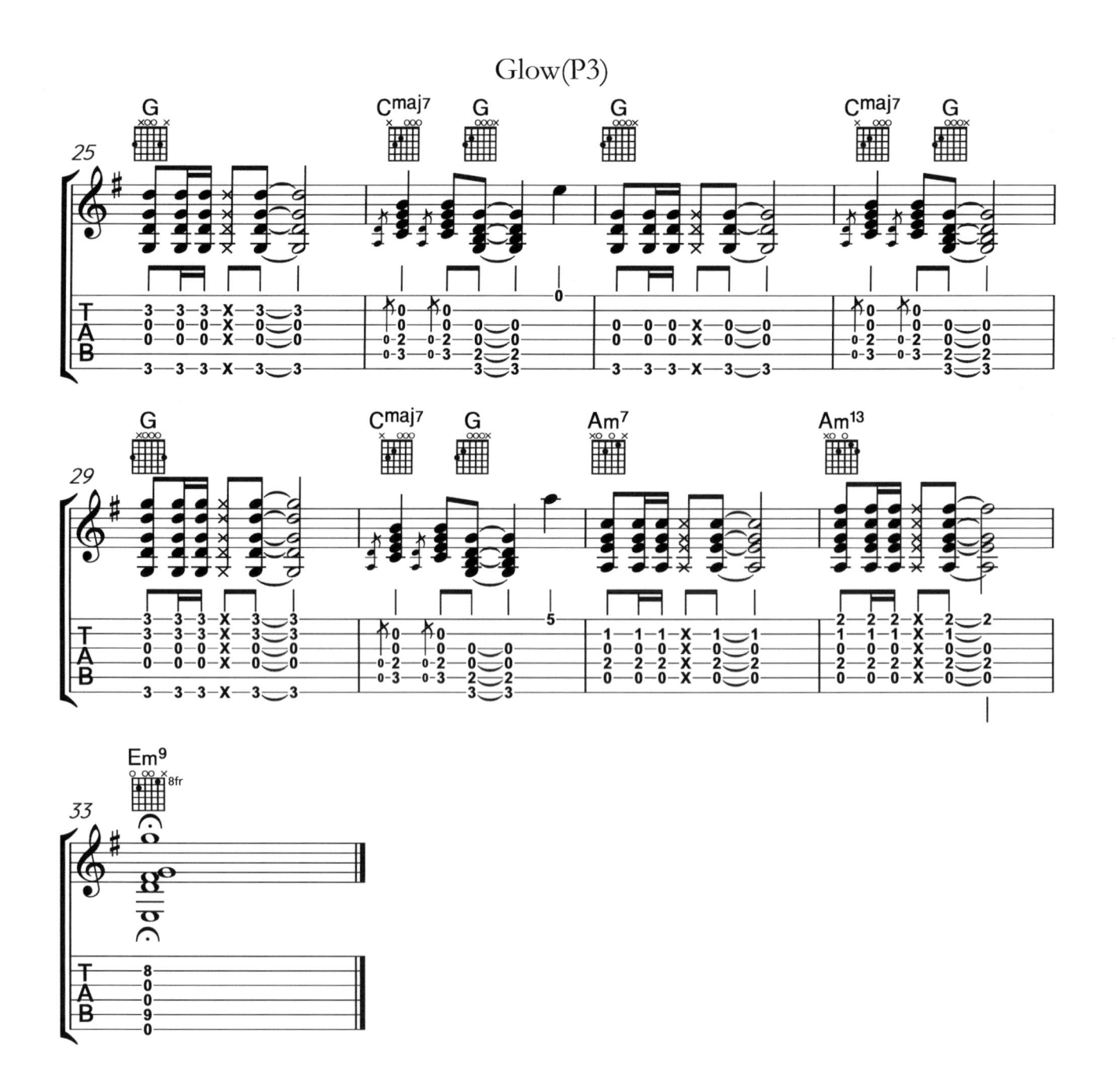

8) Quirky (Grade 5 level)

Melodic Minor Harmony

(Note: here the melodic minor scale is the same ascending and descending)

Just like in Aragón (Piece #5), we are going to look at the harmony and how triads and chords can be derived from the scales. In the same way triads and chords can be built from the major scale, exactly the same process can be applied to the melodic minor scale in order to create some really interesting sounds and chords. Study#8 covers the basics of how these chords are constructed and how to play them.

Study #8

Note: Make sure you have had a look through study#5 before trying Study#8.

Chromatic Scale

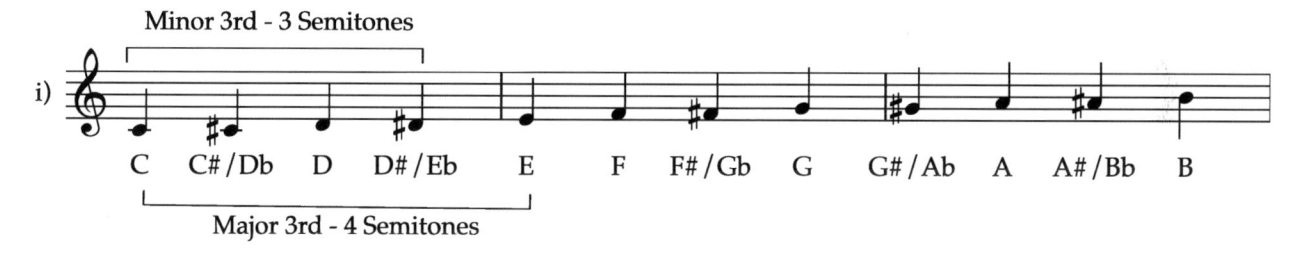

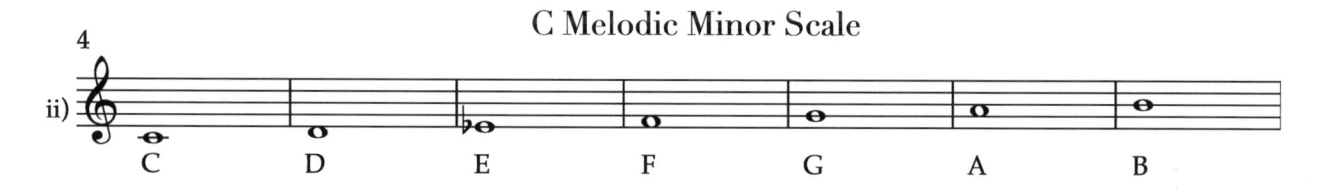

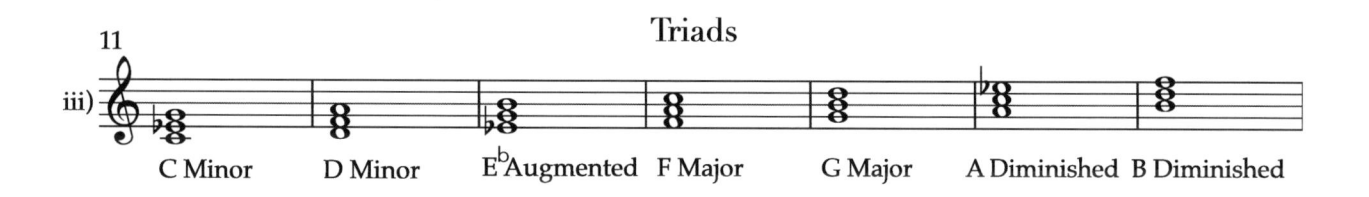

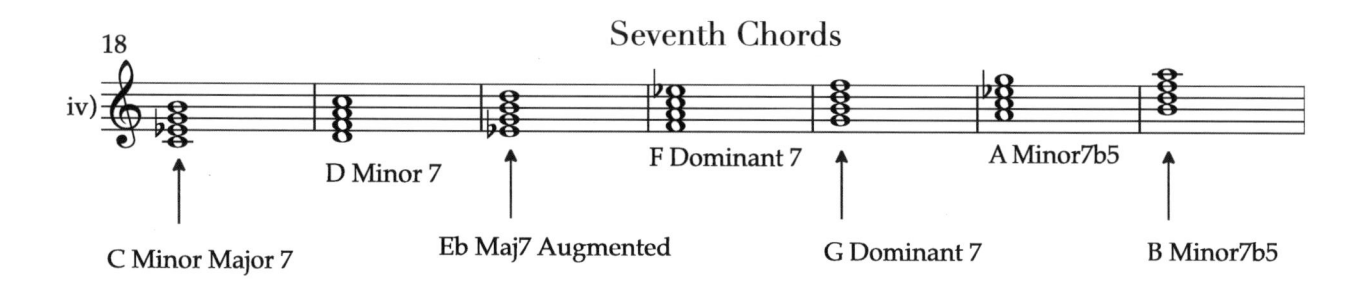

i) C C#/Db D D#/Eb E F F#/Gb G G#/Ab A A#/Bb B

Minor 3rd - 3 Semitones
Major 3rd - 4 Semitones

C Melodic Minor Scale

ii) C D E F G A B

Triads

iii) C Minor, D Minor, Eb Augmented, F Major, G Major, A Diminished, B Diminished

Seventh Chords

iv) C Minor Major 7, D Minor 7, Eb Maj7 Augmented, F Dominant 7, G Dominant 7, A Minor7b5, B Minor7b5

The way we put together chords from the melodic minor scale is exactly the same way as we construct them from the melodic minor scale i.e Root + 3rd + 5th. So take the note C (Root), count up two notes in the scale in the scale to the Eb (3rd) and a further two notes up to the G (5th).

C   Eb   G   = C Minor Triad

This time how many semitones are between the root and the 3rd (C to Eb)? It's only 3. So this is a minor third. In the major scale it was C to E which is 4 semitones making a major third, hence C Major triad for the C major scale.

In the same way we can construct triads on all of the notes from the C melodic minor scale. In example iii), you can see we get a totally different set of triads.

QUIZ

1) How many minor triads can be derived from the melodic minor scale?
2) How many major triads can be derived from the melodic minor scale?
3) How many diminished triads can be derived from the melodic minor scale?

- Now we will add another note to the triad chord to make it a seventh chord (An extra note a 3rd up from the top note of the triad e.g. C,Eb,G adds a B...Counting two notes up the melodic minor scale from G arrives at B).
- Here we have some different chord types e.g. Eb major 7th Augmented.

	I	II	III	IV	V	VI	VII
Triads.	C minor	D minor	Eb Augmented	F major	G major	A diminished	B diminished
7th Chords.	C Minor -Major 7th	D minor 7	Eb Major 7 -Augmented	F Dominant 7	G dominant 7	A half-dim	B half-dim
Symbol.	CMinΔ7 C-Δ7	DMin7 D-7	EbΔ+ EbΔAug	F7	G7	Amin7b5 Aø7	Bmin7b5 Bø7

(Note: There are further descriptions you can add to the chord symbols describing the chords in more detail..e.g.F7#11 but for now knowing these chord types as above is important. (For further study, Mark Levine's book on Jazz Theory is great)

Quirky

David Series

Ballad, Freely

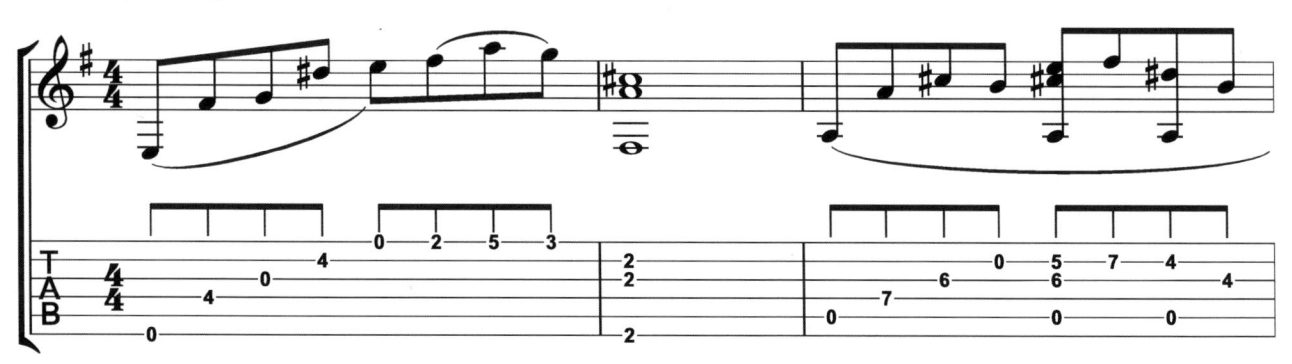

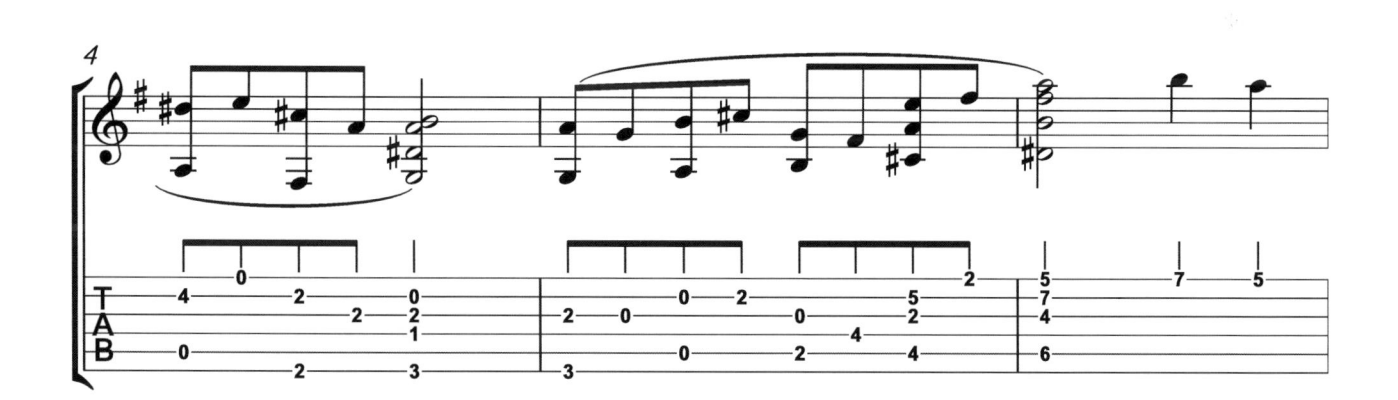

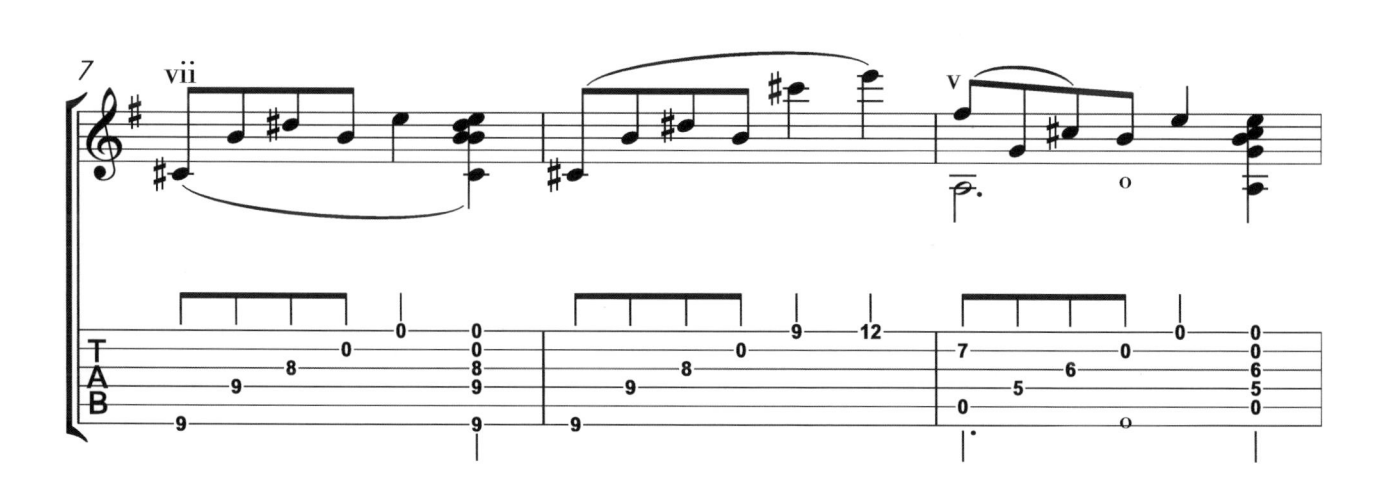

Quirky (Continued)

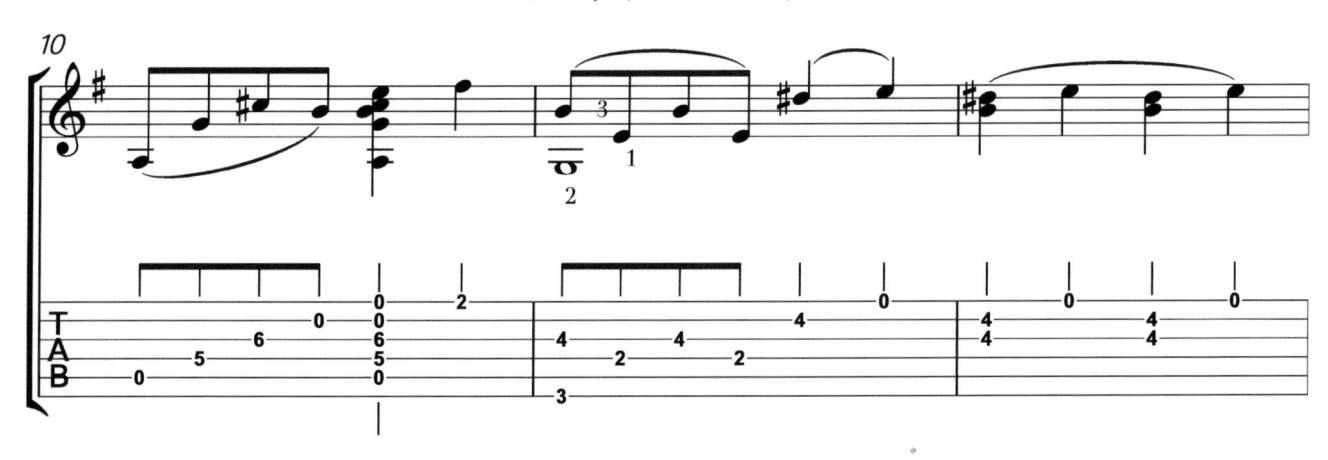

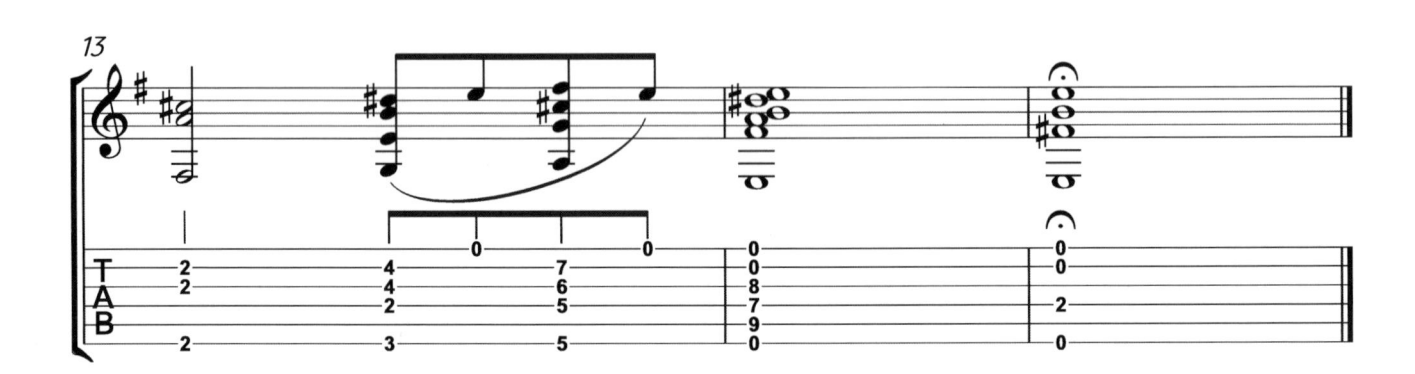

9) Twisted Blue (Grade 5/6 level)
Rhythm (Triplet feel)

This is basically a blues song with a few harmonic twists (hence the really original title!). The blues is an important part of the history of the guitar from the early days (e.g. Muddy Waters, Lightnin' Hopkins, Leadbelly, T-Bone Walker) right up to the more recent blues artists such as Eric Clapton, Stevie Ray Vaughn, BB King and many more. Broadly speaking there are two types of feel in the blues, straight or swung. This piece and study#9 focus' on the swing triplet feel, often called the shuffle in the blues context. In jazz it's called swing or triplet eigth notes. If you listen to the earlier recording of Charlie Christian (The pioneer of the electric guitar), it's almost hard to say whether it's blues or Jazz…..does it matter? Hmmmm…let's not go there just now!

Study#9

Like in study#6 I wanted to continue to use konnakol as a way of practsing and internalising rhythm. Try to work through this set of exercises in the same way as before:

1-Contiually say the subdivisions…Ta-Ki-Ta, Ta-Ki-Ta etc.

2.Then clap the notated rhythms, looping each one for a minute or so.

3.Now try the same but instead of clapping, play on your instrument with whichever chord or note your want.

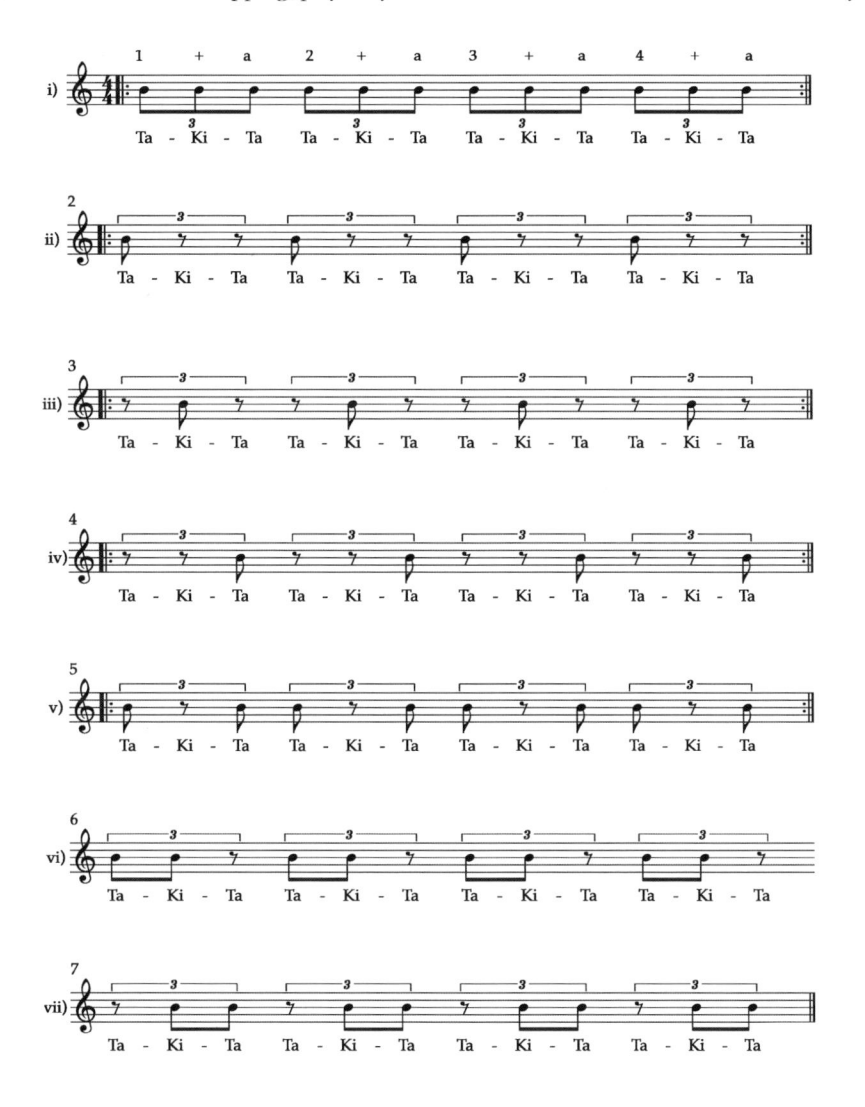

This is one part of learning the rhythmic side of the music and getting used to the shuffle or swing feel.

The other part is to listen to the music. This is SO important. Try to find recordings that you really love, it always helps in learning something if you like it! Here are some suggested albums/ musicans/ bands for blues or Jazz to listen to in trying to hear the swing/ shuffle feel. You could start by asking is the track straight or swung?

Stevie Ray Vaughn - Double Trouble

John Lee Hooker - Boom Boom

Freddie King - Texas Cannonball

Muddy Waters - At Newport 1960

Eric Clapton - From the Cradle

BB King - Live at The Regal

Chuck Berry - St Louis to Liverpool

Charlie Christian - With The Benny Goodman Sextet And Orchestra

Wes Montgomery - Boss Guitar

John Scofield - John Scofield plays the music of Ray Charles

Count Basie - The Atomic Mr Basie

Oscar Peterson - Night Train

Kenny Burrell - Midnight Blue

These are just a tiny percentage of all the artists and albums out there but ones I love to listen to again and again.

Twisted Blue

David Series

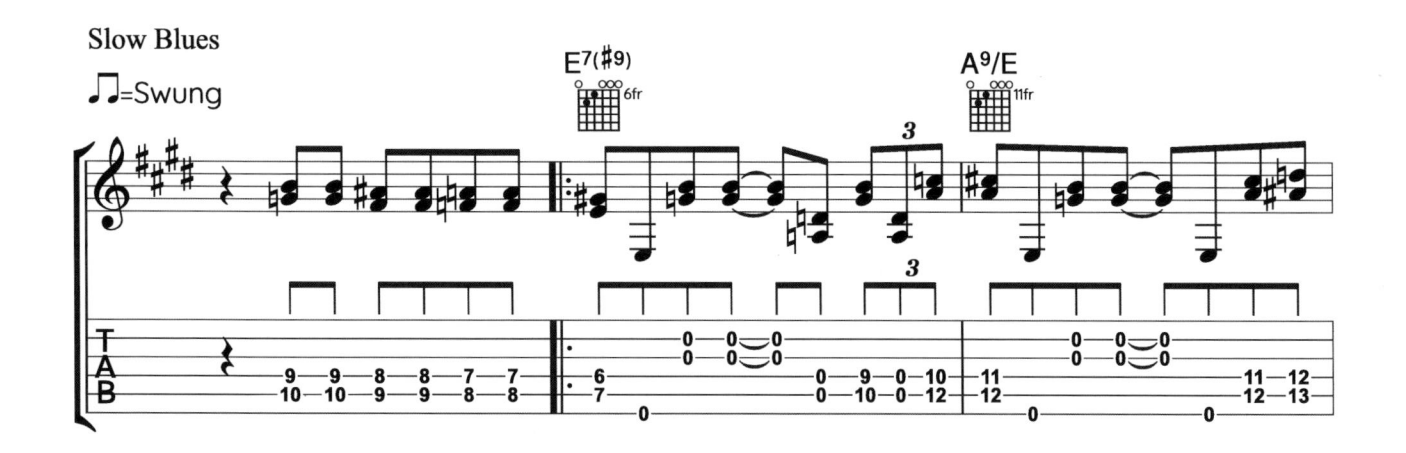

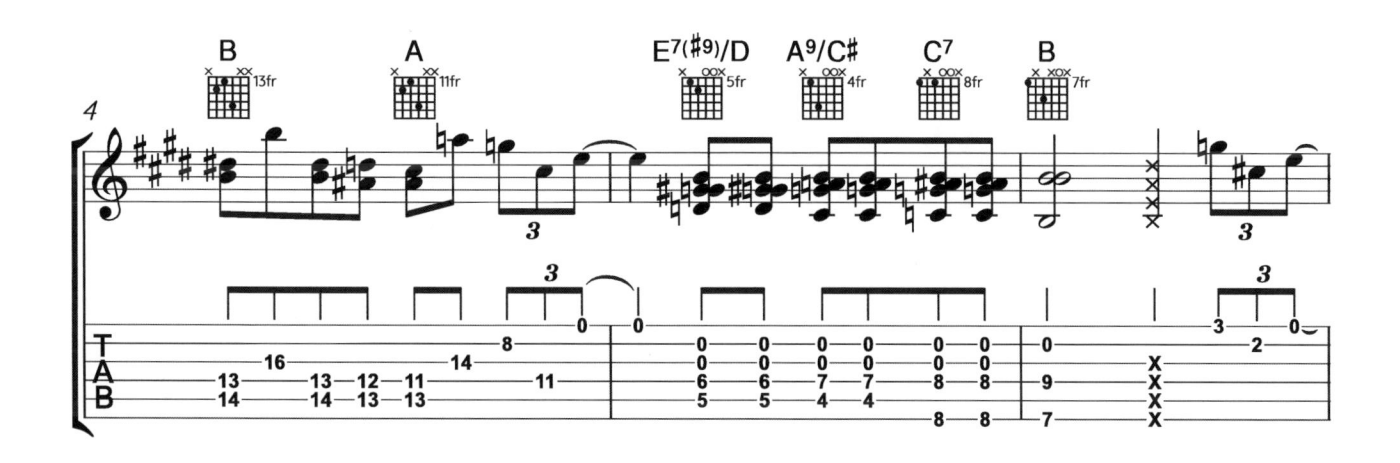

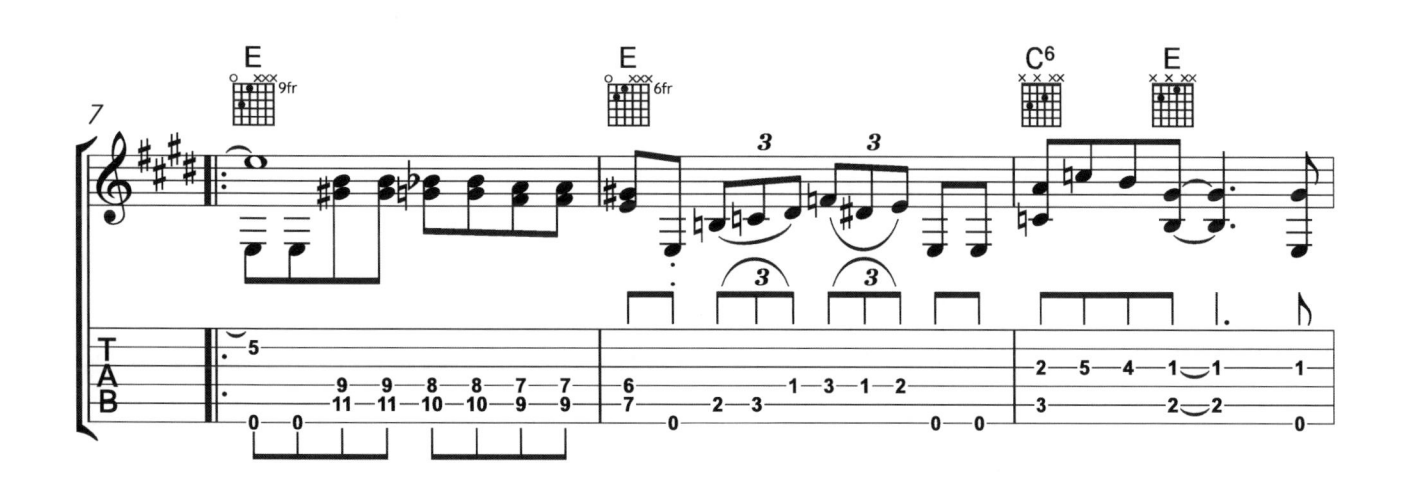

Twisted Blue (Continued)

10) Pepe of Granada (Grade 3/4 level)

Phrasing

We have all been learning to use our voice since a very young age. It is a skill we all have and have been developing for years. This piece and study#10 try to convey and work on the idea that phrasing musically can be just like speaking sentences. This piece can be played freely and I want you to try and play it in different ways, all led by your voice and the way you phrase. You don't need to be able to sing to do this!

This is just working towards trying to show you what your voice instrument connection is, that it exists in everyone and can really help you to phrase more strongly.

- Say the sounds below the notes and either make them long or short as described above.
- Then vary the speed of the whole thing

Study #10

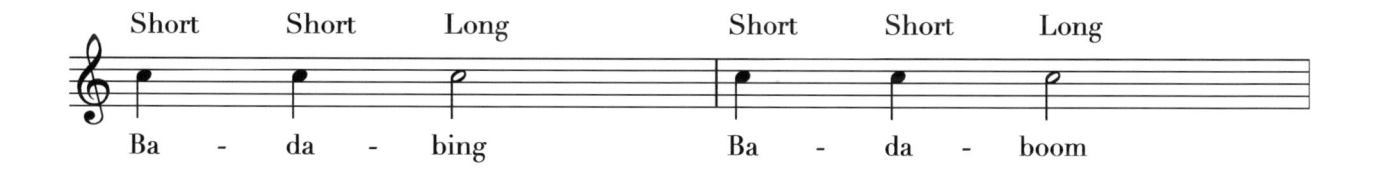

Short   Short   Long   Short   Short   Long
Ba - da - bing   Ba - da - boom

Same again but faster

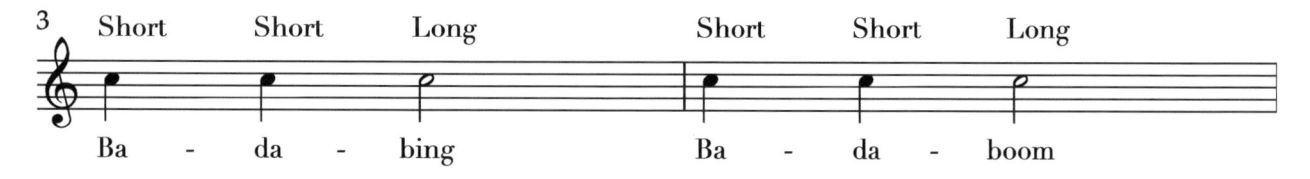

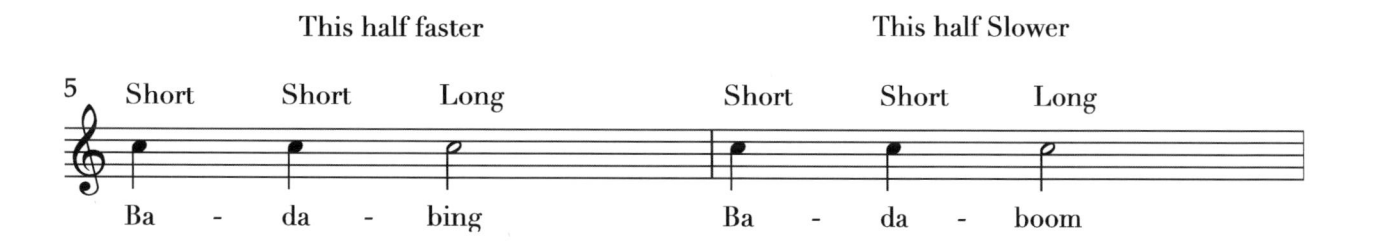

Short   Short   Long   Short   Short   Long
Ba - da - bing   Ba - da - boom

This half faster   This half Slower

Short   Short   Long   Short   Short   Long
Ba - da - bing   Ba - da - boom

Now try the same, this time with your guitar. When you come to learn Pepe of Granada…try to implement this idea. Or you could use it on any piece you already know, trying to vocalise the rhythms or notes…..you don't need to be a great singer!

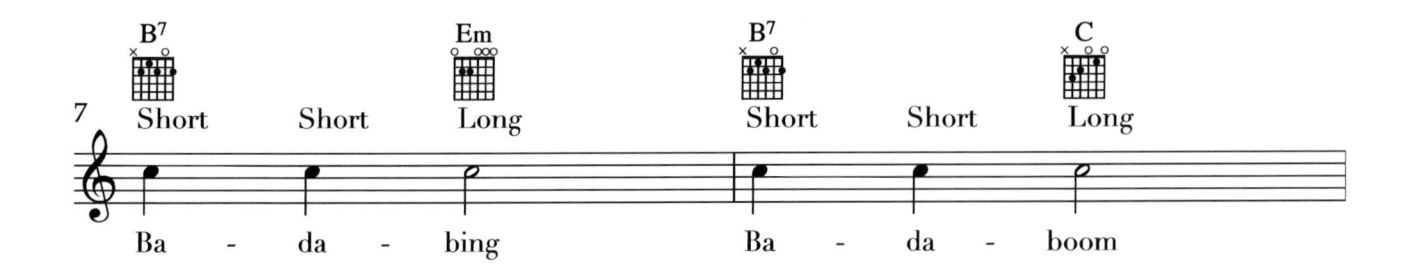

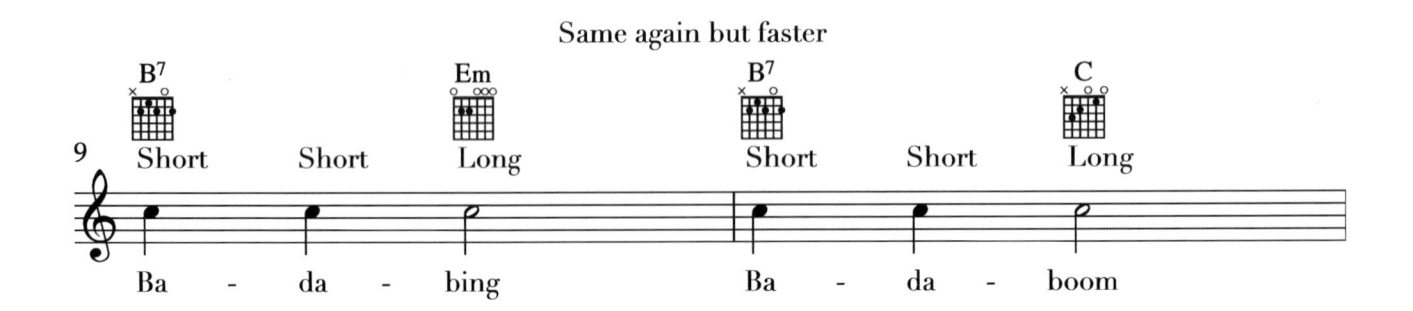

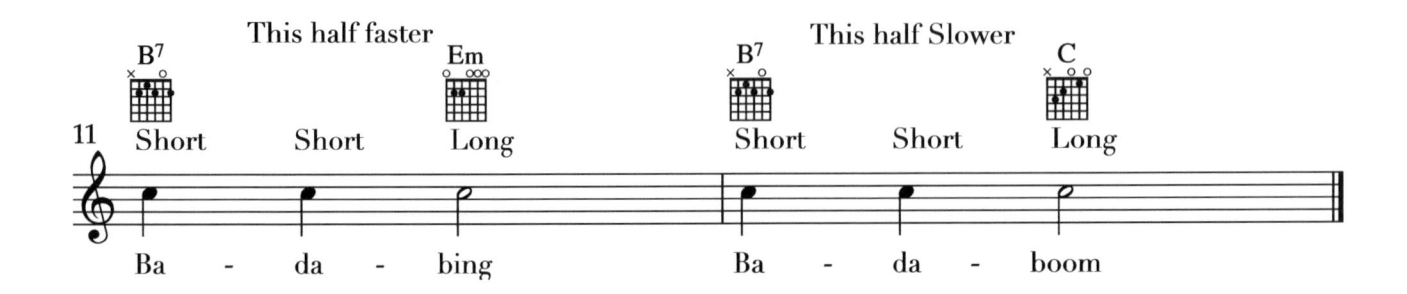

B7	Em	B7	C
Short Short Long		Short Short Long	
Ba - da - bing		Ba - da - boom	

Same again but faster

B7	Em	B7	C
Short Short Long		Short Short Long	
Ba - da - bing		Ba - da - boom	

This half faster — *This half Slower*

B7	Em	B7	C
Short Short Long		Short Short Long	
Ba - da - bing		Ba - da - boom	

Pepe of Granada

David Series

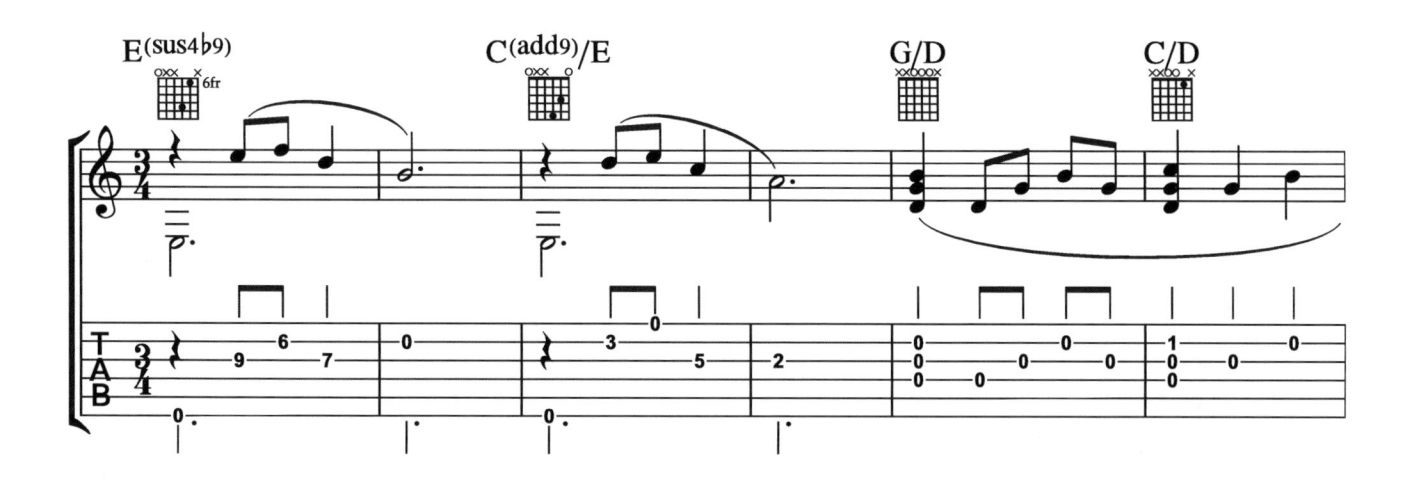

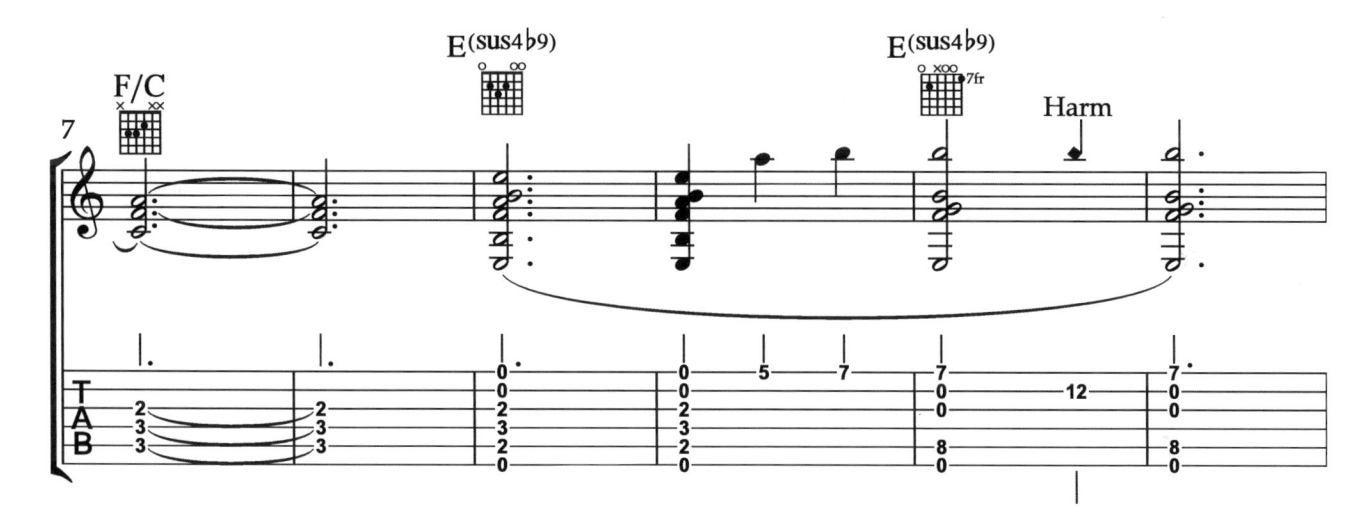

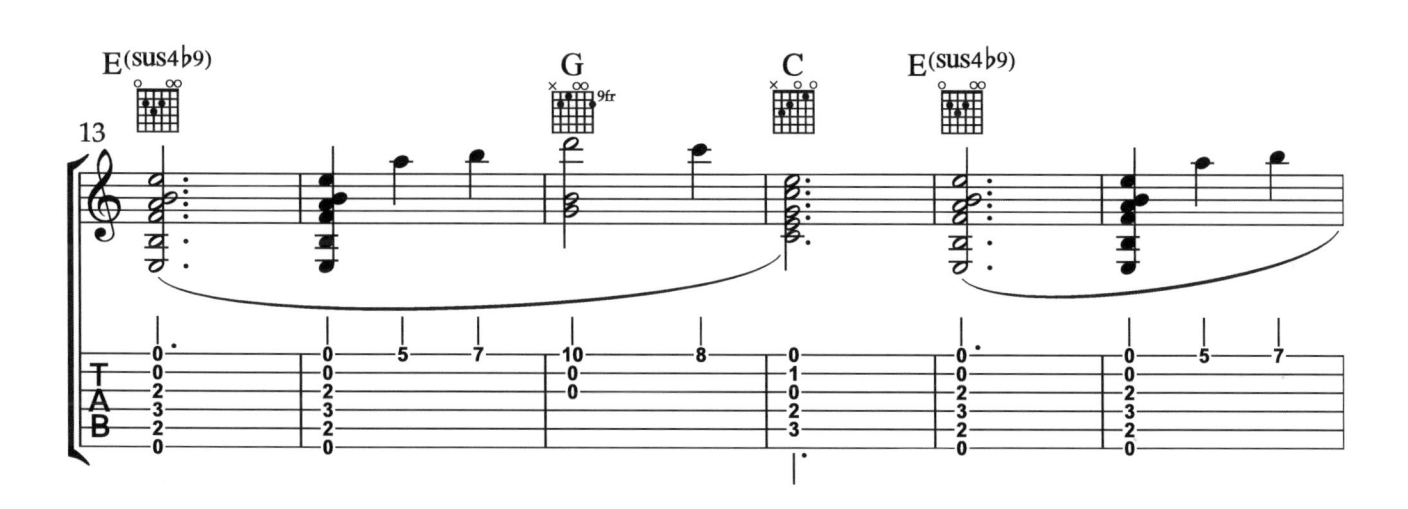

Pepe Of Granada (Continued)

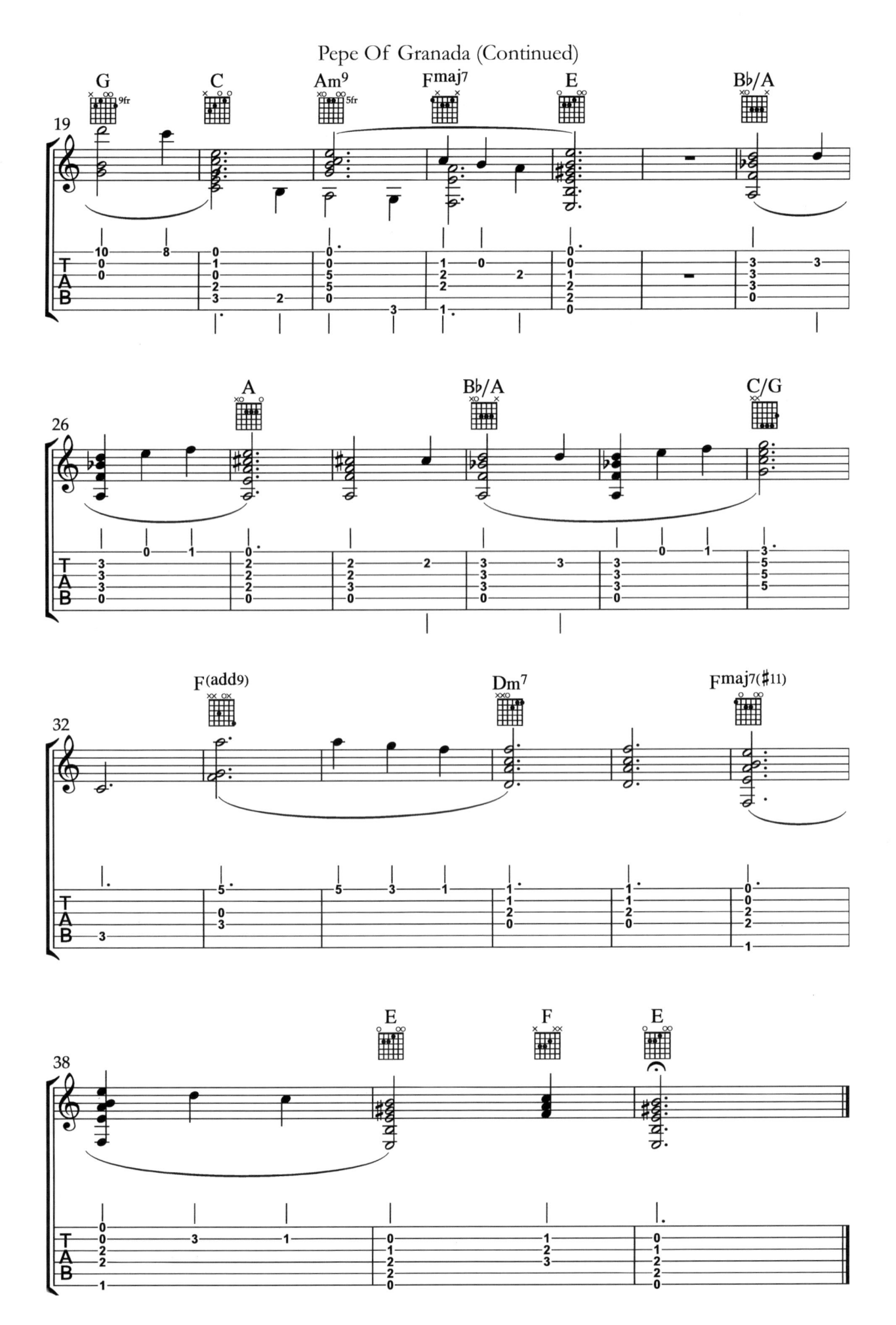

11) Shady (Grade 5)

Modal playing and theory

This study takes a look at modal harmony. The most famous example of modal playing in Jazz is Miles Davis' album Kind of Blue. Here they experimented with different sounds created by writing and improvising with certain modes derived from the major scale. In study#10 we break down the major scale in a slightly different way than before and learn about modal harmony.

Study #11

C Major Scale (Ionian - 1st Mode)

D Dorian - 2nd Mode

E Phrygian - 3nd Mode

F Lydian - 4th Mode

G Mixolydian - 5th Mode

A Aeolian - 6th Mode

B Locrian - 7th Mode

The Major scale has another name, the Ionian scale. This was the name given by Heinrich Glarean (Swiss) in 1547. The other 6 modes of the major scale have names from ancient Greek musical terminology. A mode is basically playing the notes from one particular parent scale, but starting from a different degree of the scale. So for example C major is C D E F G A B C….if we start on the D and go to the next D, an octave higher we get D E F G A B C D (So only using notes from the C Major scale). This is the second mode of the major scale, also known as Dorian. If we do the same from each degree of the scale we get:

1st Mode - Ionian   C D E F G A B C
2nd Mode - Dorian   D E F G A B C D
3rd Mode - Phrygian   E F G A B C D E
4th Mode - Lydian   F G A B C D E F
5th Mode - Mixolydian   G A B C D E F G
6th Mode - Aeolian.   A B C D E F G A
7th Mode - Locrian.   B C D E F G A B

There's is plenty information out there going into more detail on these modes and this is just an introduction. The important thing to note is that they all have their own distinct sound. Play these scales or get your teacher to play them to you, what words spring to mind to describe each sound?! Keep them personal to you, whatever comes to mind!

BREAK FOR SOME INSPIRATION!!......

"Works of Art Make Rules, Rules do not make works of art " - Claude Debussy

"I can't understand why people are frightened of new ideas. I'm frightened of the old ones." – John Cage

"I would rather write 10,000 notes than a single letter of the alphabet."
Ludwig van Beethoven

"One good thing about music, when it hits you, you feel no pain." Bob Marley

"At the risk of sounding hopelessly romantic, love is the key element. I really love to play with different musicians who come from different cultural backgrounds."
John McLaughlin

"Music doesn't lie" Jimi Hendrix

"The *music* is not in the notes, but in the silence between" Wolfgang Amadeus Mozart

"You've got to learn your instrument, then you practice, practice, practice. Then when you finally get on the band stand, just get up there and wail" Charlie Parker

"If I were not a physicist, I would probably be a musician. I often think in music. I live my daydreams in music. I see my life in terms of music." Albert Einstein

Shady

Funky

David Series

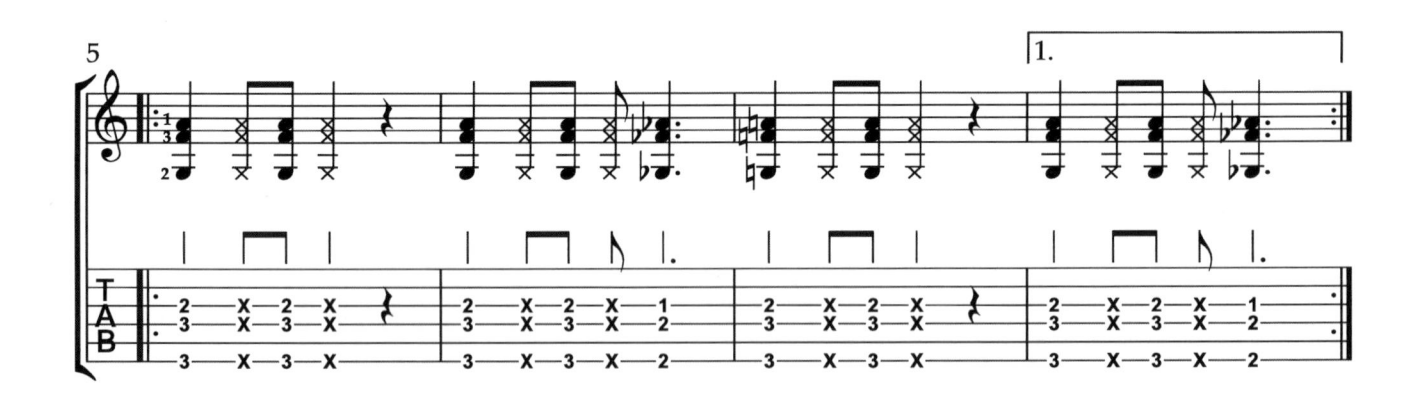

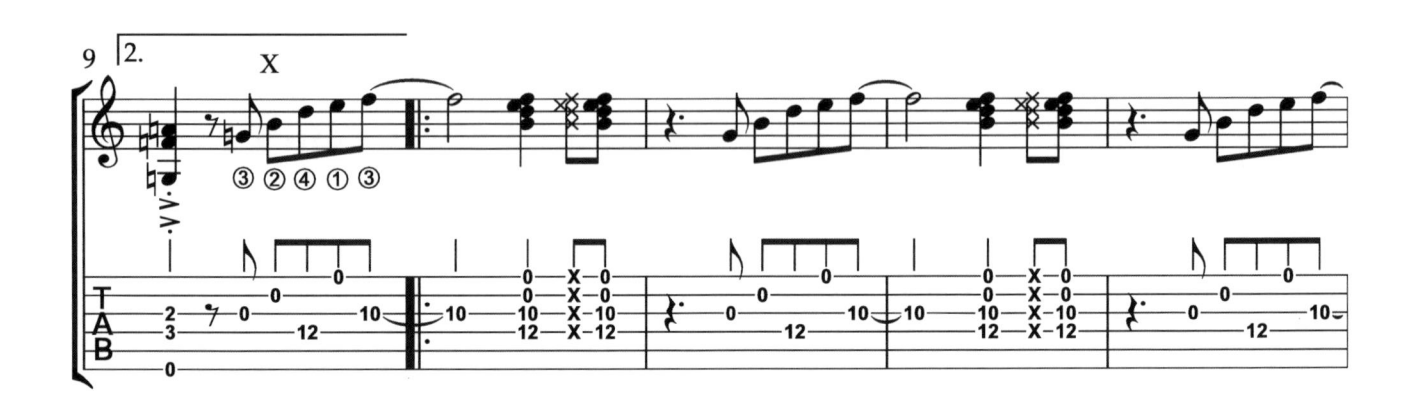

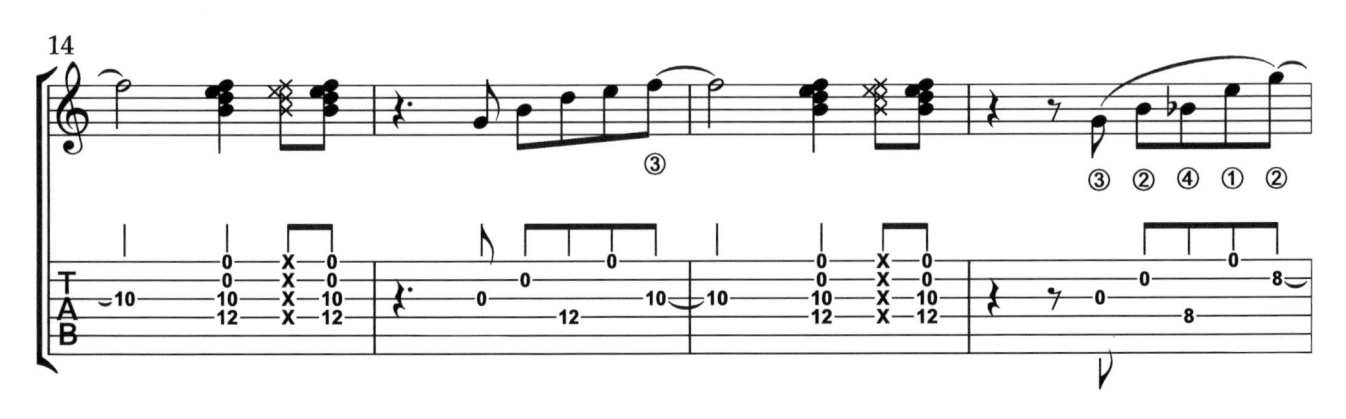

Shady (Continued)

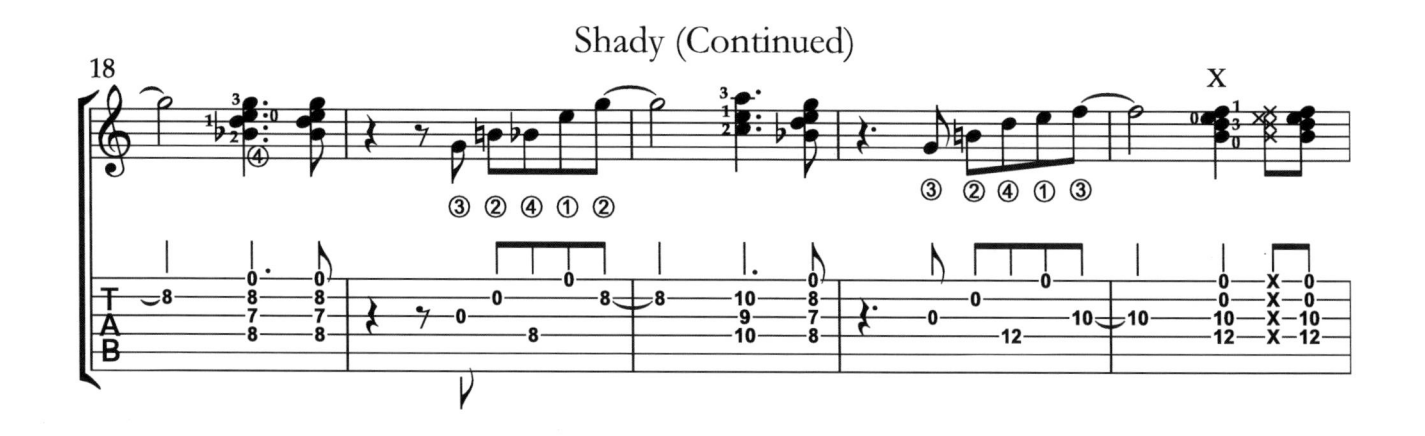

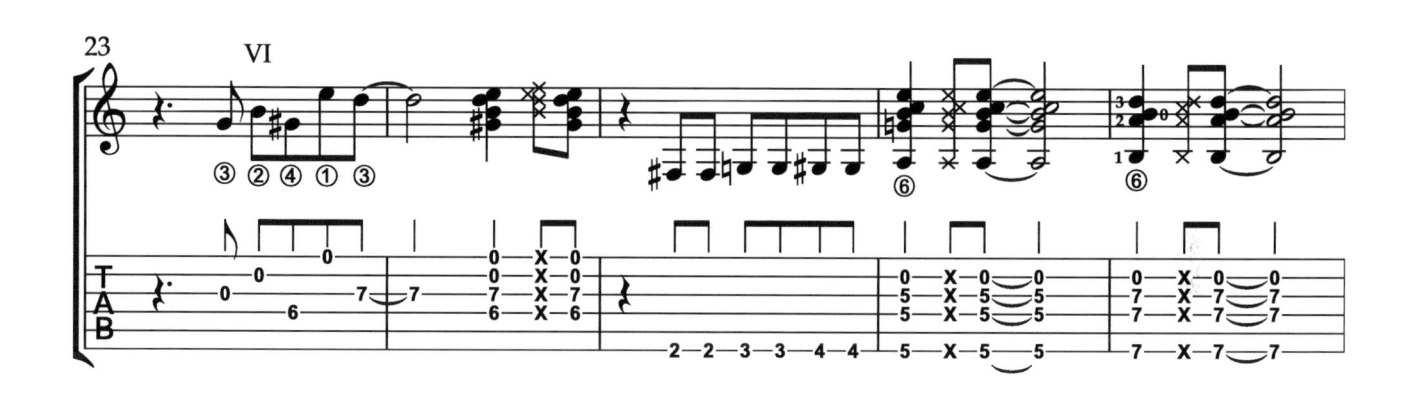

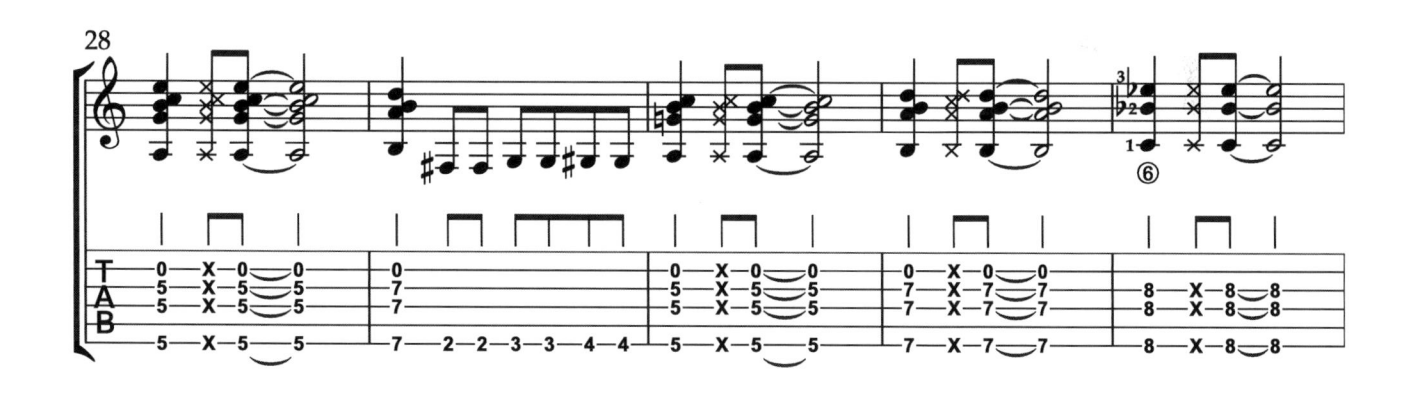

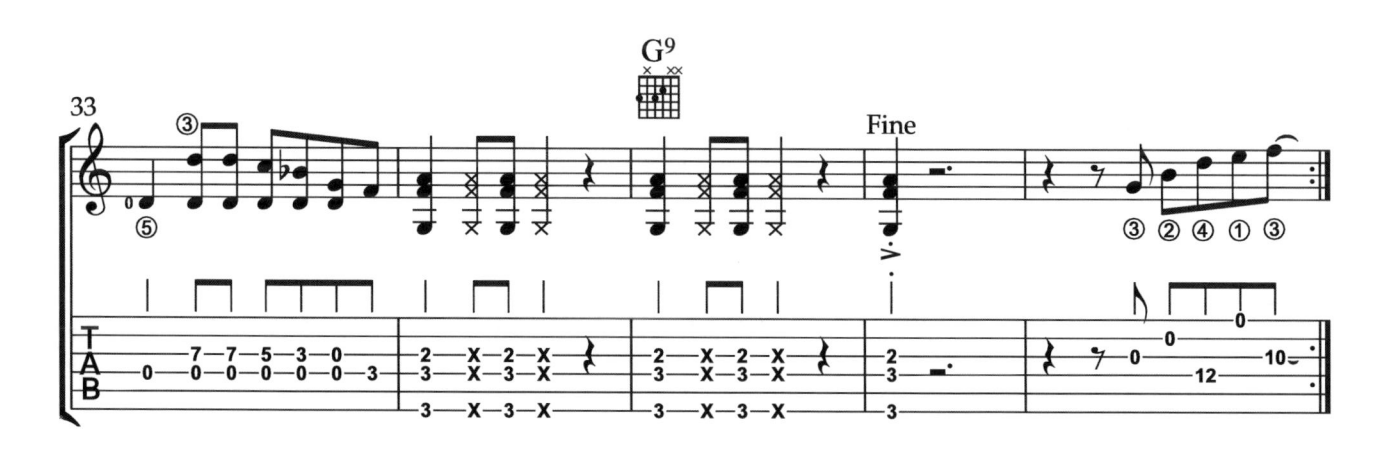

12) Coloured Stones (Grade 6/7)

Right-hand technique (Finger-picking and Tremolo)

Developing the right-hand technique can give you so many ideas and tools to be creative with as well as making your playing stronger and giving you more control. This composition and study takes a look at using both finger-picking and tremolo playing. Study#12a and 12b are an introduction to practising tremolo.

Study #12a

- These exercises should be practiced with a metronome, first at a speed which is easy for you and then gradually push the tempo up a little each time you practise.
- Where it starts to feel out of control or tense or you are missing notes, this is your limit. Make a note of this tempo and practise a bit below it for a while until you feel really in control at the slower speed before trying to move the tempo higher again.
- Over time, just a few minutes a day, you will see you slowly start to have more control and dexterity with your right hand.

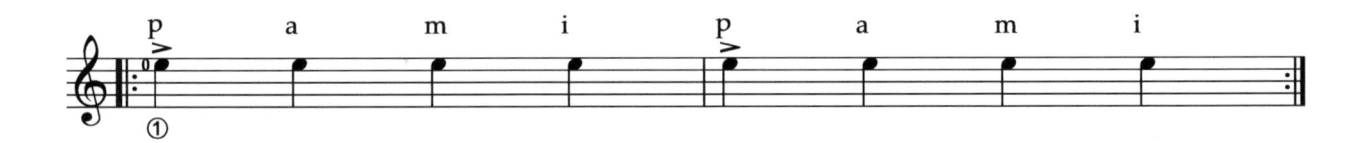

Study #12b

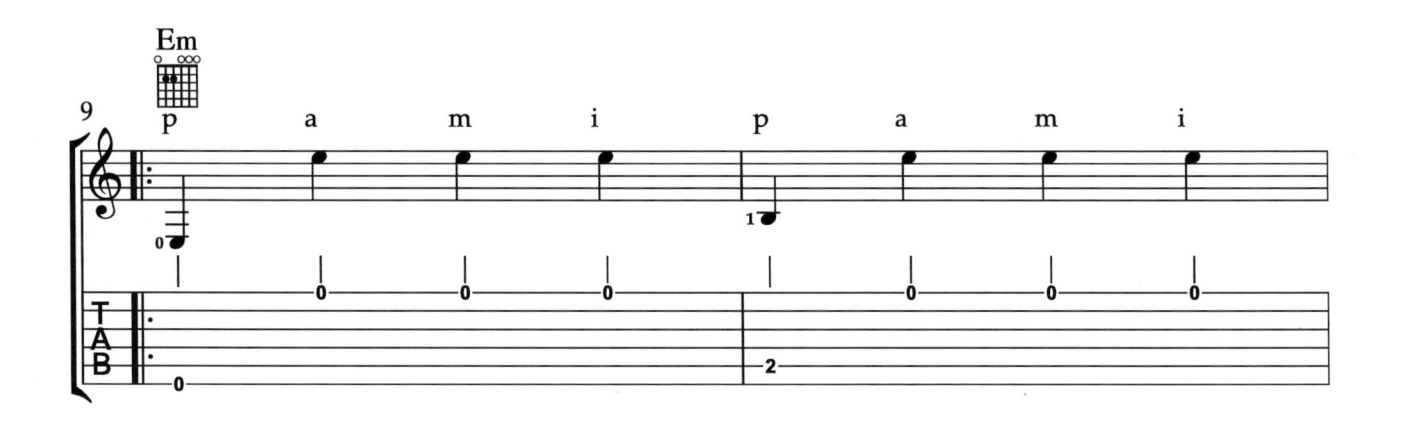

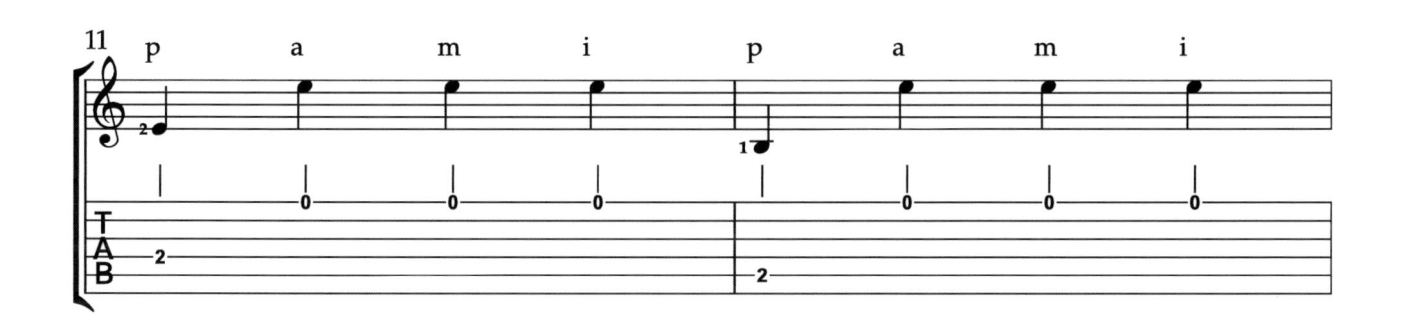

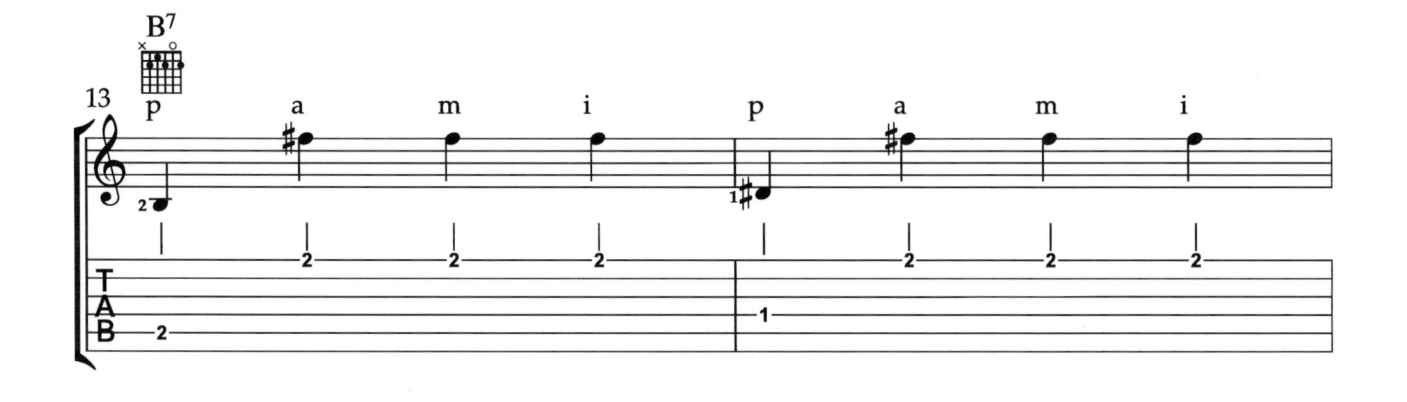

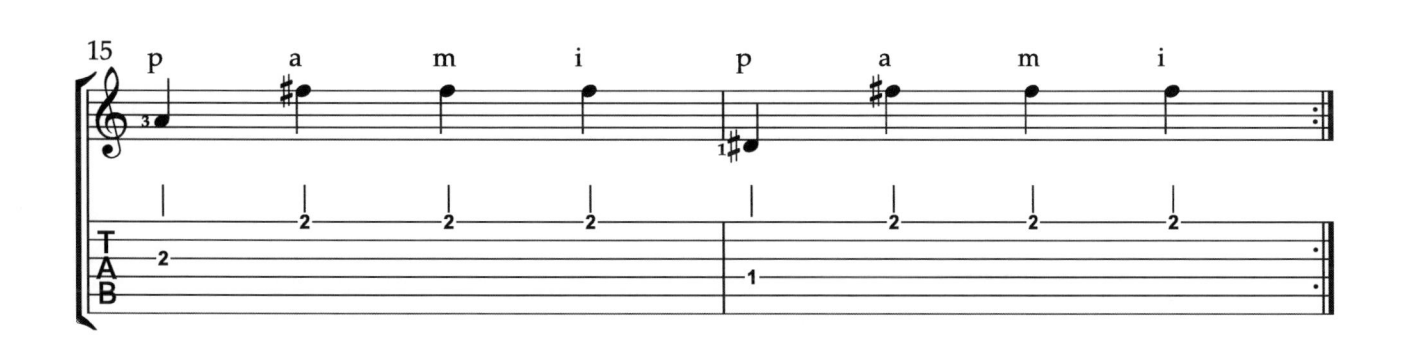

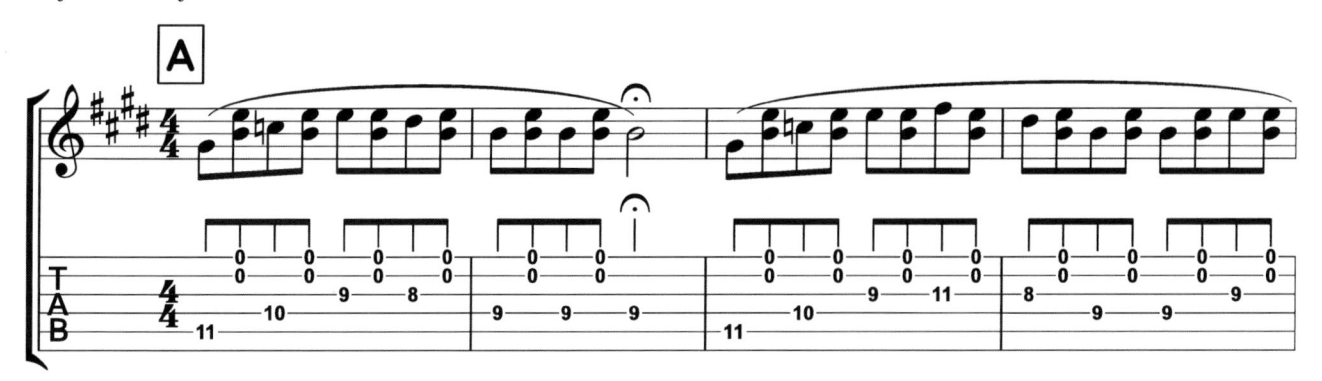

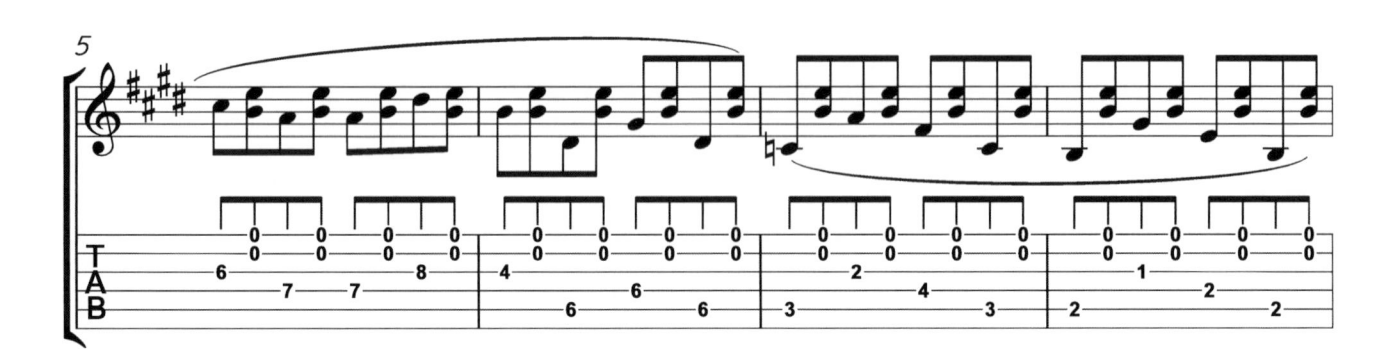

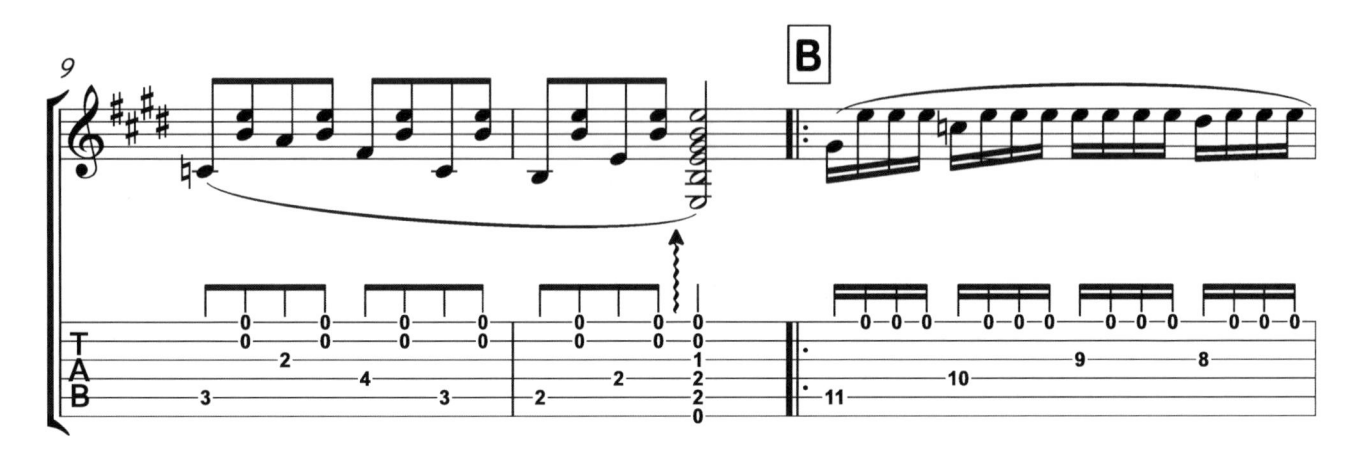

Coloured Stones

David Series

Let notes ring,
Played Freely

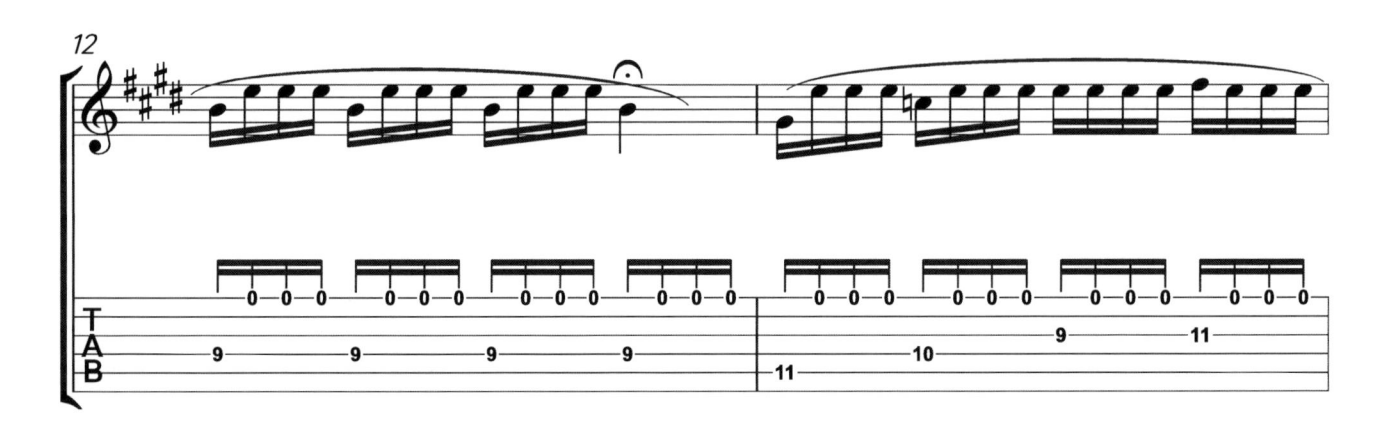

Coloured Stones (P2)

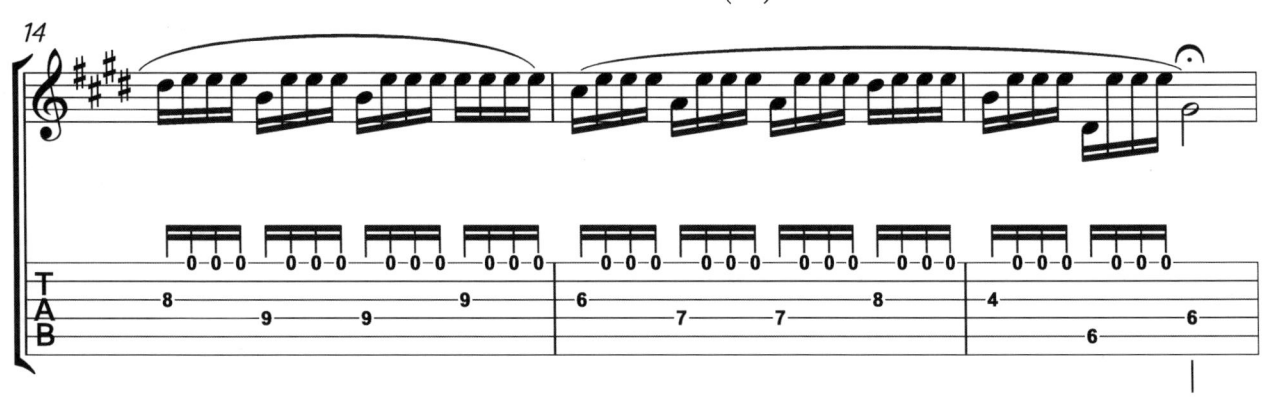

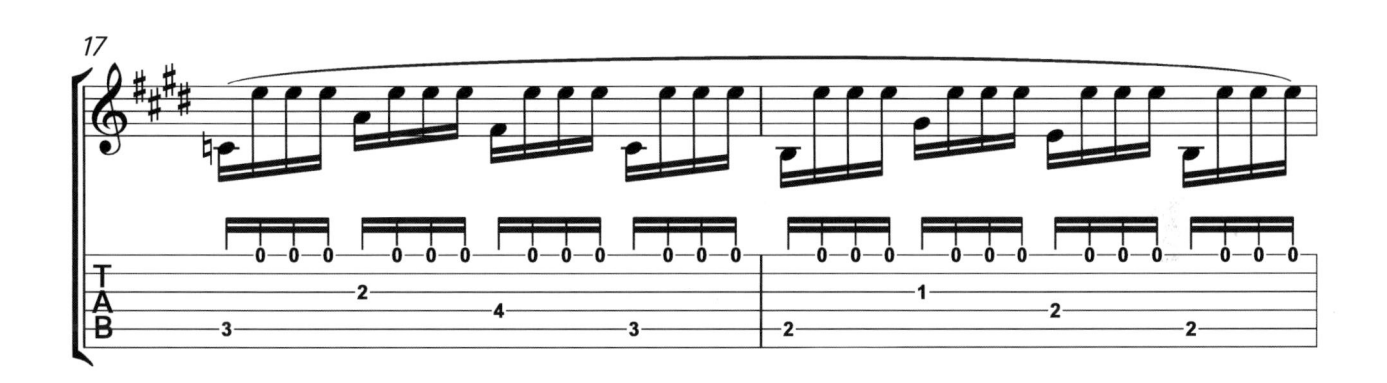

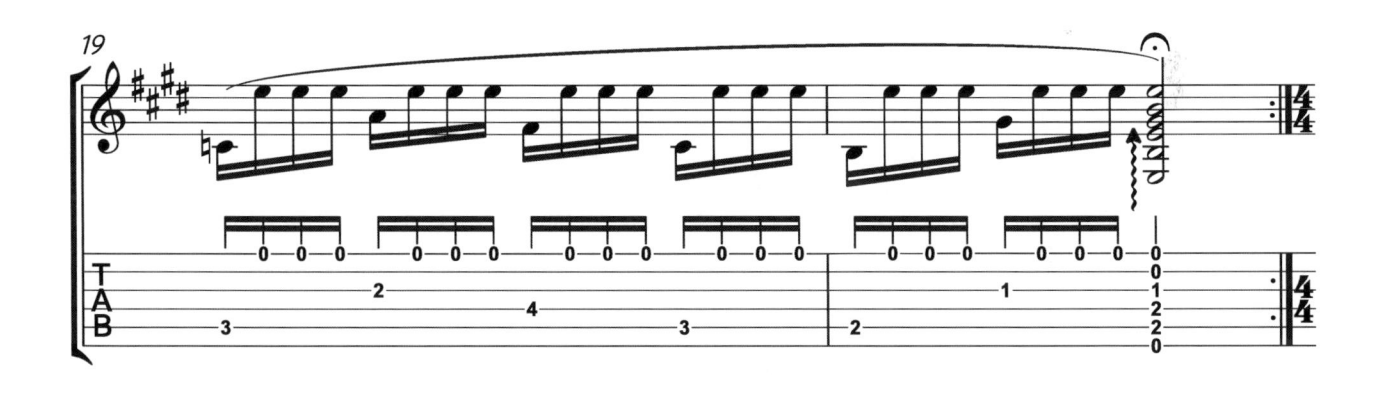

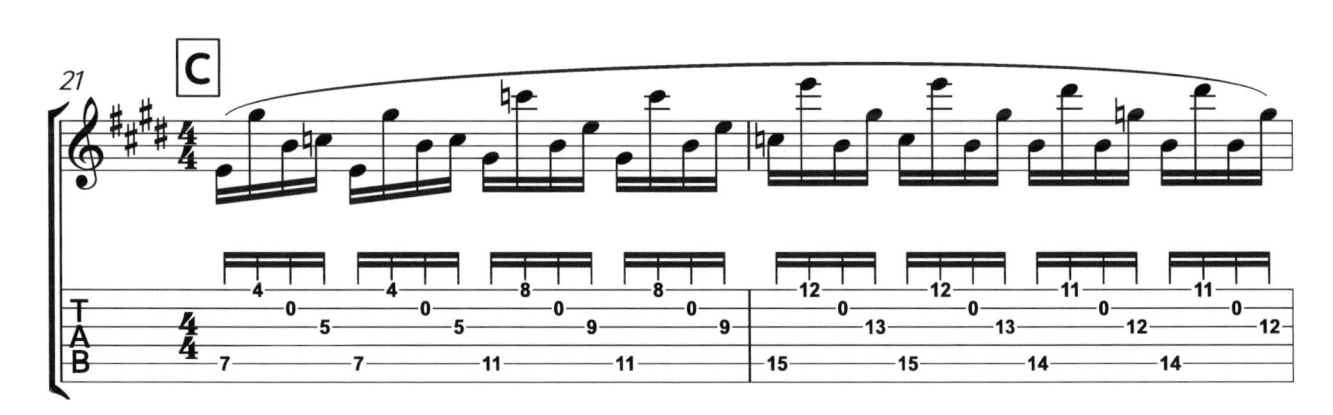

Coloured Stones (P3)

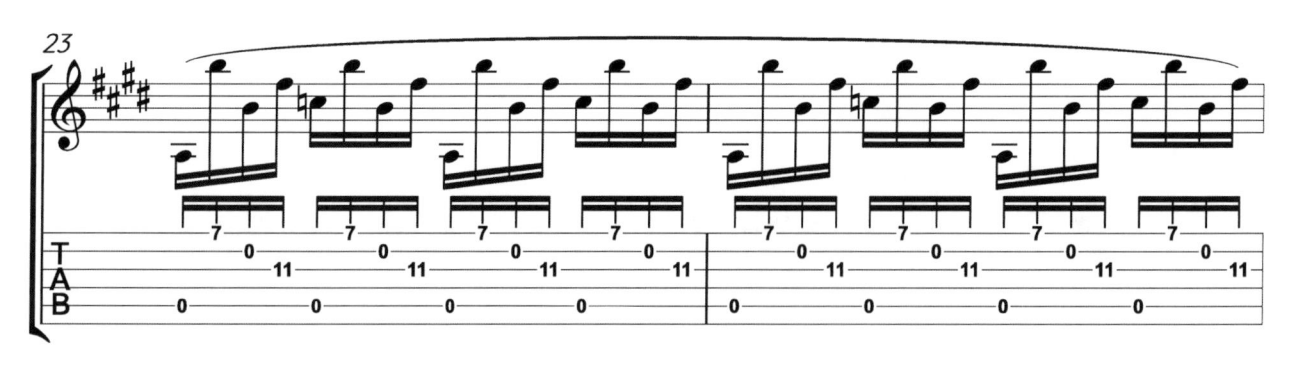

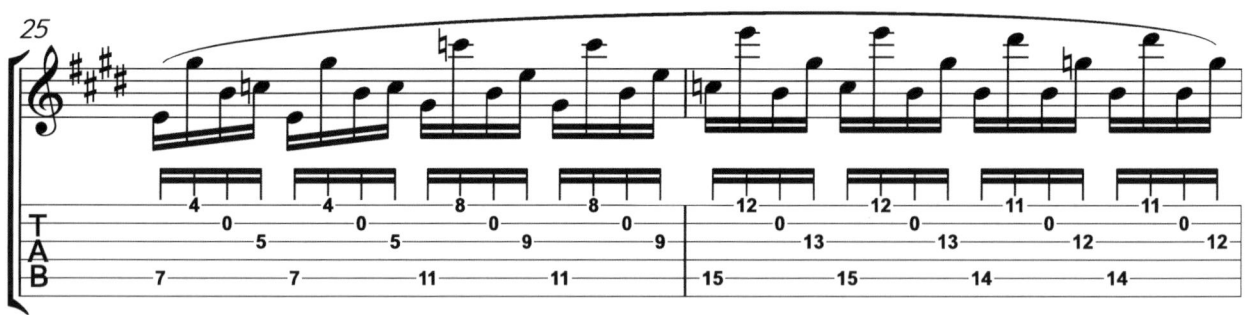

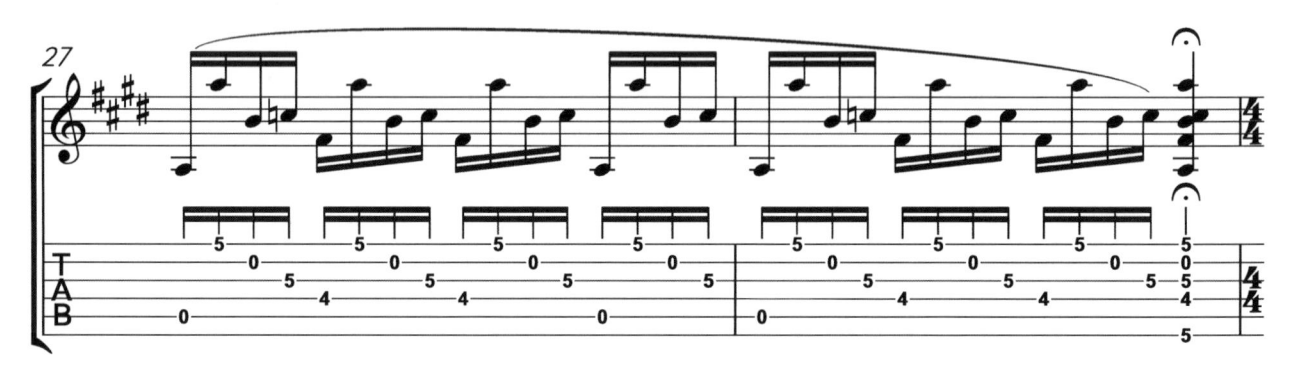

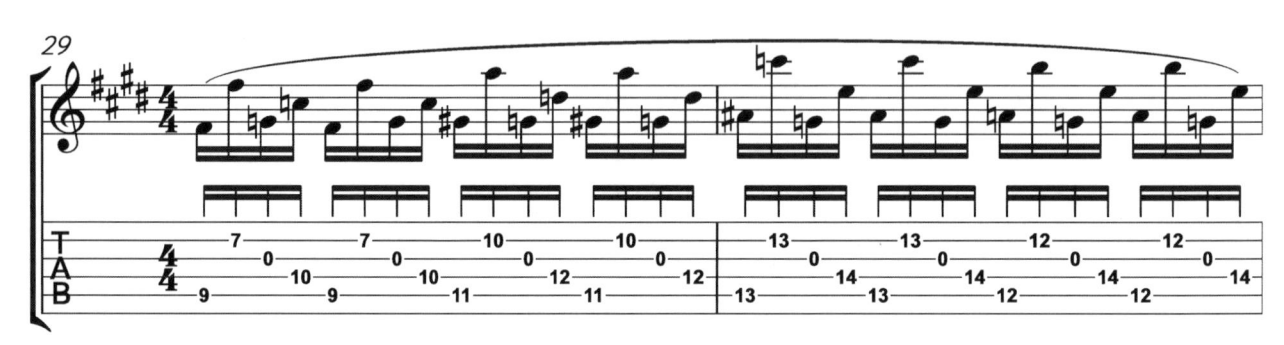